HARTFORD
IN WORLD WAR I

HARTFORD
IN WORLD WAR I

DAVID DRURY

THE
History
PRESS

Published by The History Press
Charleston, SC
www.historypress.net

Copyright © 2015 by David Drury
All rights reserved

Front cover, bottom left: YMCA field secretary Frank E. Johnson of Hartford, *Connecticut State Library*.

First published 2015

Manufactured in the United States

.

ISBN 978.1.62619.796.1

Library of Congress Control Number: 2015949271

In memory of my sister, Denise,
who urged me to write a book

Contents

Acknowledgements

My fascination with the Great War began almost a half century ago. Perhaps it was from reading Barbara Tuchman's *The Guns of August* in high school. Or maybe it was triggered by British historians of the period, like A.J.P. Taylor or B.H. Liddell Hart, whose work I read in college. Whatever the cause, the effects were long-standing, reaching a pinnacle in 1997, when I had the opportunity to visit the western front: Ypres, the Somme, the Chemin-des-Dames, the Marne Valley, Verdun, the Meuse-Argonne and several of the pristine cemeteries and monuments maintained by the American Battle Monuments Commission. When my piece about the trip was published in the travel section of my newspaper, the *Hartford Courant*, I could say I had written something about the Great War and cross it off my bucket list.

Then in late 2013, I received an e-mail from Tabitha Dulla, a commissioning editor with The History Press. Tabitha had read some articles I had written for the *Courant* on topics related to Connecticut's participation in the Civil War and asked whether I had any interest in writing a local history book. Having done a bit of research previously on Connecticut during World War I, I was aware that the Connecticut State Library maintained a wealth of holdings from the period. With the centennial of the Great War approaching and aware that the subject was something of a black hole in popular consciousness—an interlude between the Civil War and World War II that inspired highly costumed British period pieces for public television—I thought I had my subject.

So began an eighteen-month project made possible with the help and guidance of many people and the remarkable advances in digital technology that allow a researcher access to hard-to-find documents and publications via home computer. Much of the flesh and bone of the book was developed from archives and materials available at or through the Connecticut State Library. My gratitude to the members of state librarian Kendall F. Wiggin's History & Genealogy staff and, in particular, to Christine Pittsley, coordinator for *Remembering World War I: Sharing History/Preserving Memories*, a project undertaken by the Connecticut State Library, the University of Connecticut and Historypin to create a permanent, publicly accessible record of the state's World War I experience. This book would not have taken the shape it did without Christine's help.

Outside the state library, I received willing, enthusiastic support from research assistants and archivists, museum curators, librarians and leaders of local historical societies. Thanks go out to Pat Watson at the New Britain Public Library; Richard Ring, head curator of the Watkinson Library at Trinity College; Mary Jane Springman of the Simsbury Free Public Library; Barbara Strong of the Simsbury Historical Society; Laura Smith at the Thomas J. Dodd Research Center at the University of Connecticut; the Manchester Historical Society; and the staff at Waterman Research Center of the Connecticut Historical Society. Karen Winslow Hudkins, director of the New Britain Industrial Museum, opened a window into the Hardware City's manufacturing past. Nancy Macaione, an Aetna Company archivist, photocopied a file of company wartime documents. Jessica Jenkins, collections curator of the Litchfield Historical Society, shared images from its poster collection. Melanie Anderson Bourbeau of the Hill-Stead Museum provided materials documenting Theodate Pope's ordeal aboard the *Lusitania*. Thanks also go to Robert Ellis of the West Haven (Connecticut) Veterans Museum for the brilliant photographic images from the museum's collection, the Rau-Locke American Legion Post 8 and the Legion's Connecticut historian Frazier Brinley. Finally, special thanks go to Carol Denehy for her generous sharing of the holdings of the Memorial Military Museum of Bristol, begun by her late husband.

Finally, love and gratitude go to my wife, Kitty, for her patience and support.

INTRODUCTION

In July 2014, at the dawning of the centennial of the Great War, a group of scholars shared their thoughts about the cataclysmic event during a panel discussion at the National World War I Museum in Kansas City, Missouri. Dr. Chad Williams, associate professor and chairman of the Africa and Afro-American Studies Department at Brandeis University, summarized with elegant simplicity the importance of the period: "World War I was a big deal. It mattered in many ways…if I had to choose one word, I would characterize it as tragic. It was a tragic historical moment but one that was incredibly important to how we think about the world today."[1]

World War I was, indeed, a big deal, a global conflict waged on a massive industrial scale that left no one who lived through it untouched. This was true not only in Europe but also in the United States, which entered the war in April 1917 after prolonged, prosperous neutrality. The state of Connecticut had shared in the fruits of that neutrality, most prominently the gun makers and munitions manufacturers in Bridgeport, New Haven and the capital city of Hartford, where Colt's Patent Firearms Manufacturing Co. had European connections dating back to the time of Samuel Colt himself.

Colt's famous revolvers had put Hartford on the world's industrial map, but by the late nineteenth century, the city's reputation for manufacturing innovation and ingenuity had expanded well beyond gun making. Precision milling machinery and machine tools, threaded screws and sewing machines, bicycles and typewriters churned from its factories. That industrial dynamism continued into the early twentieth century, even as the ethnic makeup of

Hartford's craftsmen and shop workers broadened and diversified. Waves of newly arrived immigrants brought many nationalities, representing countries and regions on opposing sides of the European war, into the city. A similar pattern existed in the smaller Hartford County industrial centers like New Britain, Manchester, Bristol and Enfield. The region's industrial capability made it critical to the nation's war effort. During 1917–18, Hartford County factories turned out prodigious quantities of guns and munitions, mess kits and trench knives, gas masks and clothing and equipment to outfit the doughboys and America's allies.

As a wounded soldier from Bristol observed in a letter home written from his hospital bed:

> *We can't get away from Bristol products here, the brass in our shells and cartridges, the buttons and insignia of uniforms, the many implements we use. Before I was hit, I was riding down a Chateau Thierry road on an old bike I picked up in a battered town. It had a New Departure coaster brake, still good though ancient. At Vaux, on the one standing wall of a completely demolished house I saw a Sessions clock ticking away. The Cadillac Eights and the Dodge cars have New Departure bearings, so does our Delco Motor plant here at the hospital. All these things have Wallace Barnes springs in them, and that goes for the light Browning machine gun I handled as well as most of our weapons. This is also true of the new planes that are beginning to arrive.[2]*

Under the leadership of Republican governor Marcus H. Holcomb, Connecticut had begun earnestly preparing for war in February 1917, inventorying its manpower and industrial and agricultural resources and establishing a home guard for internal security. Following the declaration of hostilities, Holcomb appointed a group of leading citizens, business and financial leaders to the Connecticut State Council of Defense, which was charged with mobilizing all the state's industrial, agricultural, financial and human resources to defeat the Kaiser. Hartford became the hub of the state's wartime bureaucracy. From it, the spokes branched out through the state's eight counties to all 168 towns, where local officials and volunteers staffed the bureaus, committees and organizations like the Red Cross, YMCA, YWCA and Knights of Columbus that were so critical to the war effort.

To finance the war effort, Hartford County employers led liberty bond and war savings stamp drives, in some cases assiduously tracking individual contributions to the penny. But dollars do not fight wars. Men and women do that. About 12 percent of the more than sixty-six thousand Connecticut residents who served in the armed forces during the war lived in Hartford city. Volunteers from the state capital worked in overseas hospitals, drove ambulances and staffed canteens and recreation centers. Local doughboys with the famed Twenty-sixth "Yankee" Division were among the first American troops to reach France. Soldiers, sailors and marines from Hartford County fought with the American Expeditionary Forces from 1917 through its defining campaign in the Meuse-Argonne, which ended with the armistice on November 11, 1918.

The warriors were greeted as conquering heroes upon their return home. Parades and receptions were held in their hometowns. Posts of the newly formed American Legion were named to honor the fallen, and starting in the early 1920s, permanent memorials were erected to recognize their service and sacrifice. Some of those memorials, such as the towering obelisk at Walnut Hill Park in New Britain or the war monument on Memorial Boulevard in Bristol, remain cherished features of their communities today. Others, such as one established in Hartford's Colt Park, have disappeared. For the veterans themselves, life went on, and the thousands left grievously wounded, gassed, psychologically damaged or otherwise marred carried those scars for the rest of their days. To meet their needs, the State of Connecticut funded the relocation of the Civil War–era Fitch's Home for Soldiers from Darien in Fairfield County to the Hartford County town of Rocky Hill. The new Veterans Home and Hospital opened in 1940, one year before the nation entered an even greater, more devastating conflict.

This work attempts to convey a sense of what the War to End All Wars meant to Hartford.

HARTFORD AND THE EUROPEAN WAR, 1914

The summer of 1914 began very much like those of past years for the well-heeled upper crust of Hartford society. It was the season for shoreline retreats or travels to far-flung destinations aboard posh ocean liners and luxurious passenger trains, augmented by whatever local transport was available. These excursions sometimes assumed a manic quality. Three years earlier, in 1911, Hartford journalist and author Daniel Doane Bidwell, who had just published a book about a leisurely world tour taken the prior year, set a world record for frenetic, west-to-east globe-trotting: forty-six days, twenty-three hours and forty-five minutes.

Europe remained a favored destination. On July 1, 1914, three days after the heir to the Austro-Hungarian throne, Archduke Franz Ferdinand, and his wife, Sophie, were assassinated by Serbian nationals, Henry B. Hale, the owner and publisher of the *Weekly Gazette* of East Hartford, left for the Continent. The readers of his newspaper learned on July 3 that he and eleven traveling companions had departed Boston bound for Glasgow. The itinerary for "a jolly party of twelve, H.B. Hale, conductor" called for stopovers in Edinburgh and London before crossing the Channel. They planned to spend July 25 to 30 in the City of Lights—"doing the city in the grand Parisian style"—before proceeding to Belgium and the Netherlands. Their return voyage would take them to Halifax, Nova Scotia, before continuing south to New York by rail, arriving on August 16.[3]

The nine men and three women were living large in Paris when the rush of events made their summer vacation more exciting than they could have imagined. Hale's published account in the *Gazette* described how Austro-Hungary's declaration of war on Serbia on July 28 had left the French capital gripped by war fever: "It was nothing but war from morning until night." His party took the train to Brussels on Thursday, July 30. The next day, the group went sightseeing, making a side trip to the Waterloo battlefield, even as the local citizenry was making a frenzied run on the banks and troops were being called up to counter the threat of German invasion. Returning to their hotel, the vacationers were told that all further bookings were cancelled, so the following day, August 1, they boarded a train to Rotterdam. The trip, normally two hours, took eight. They stayed for several days, learning of the initial bloody encounters between German and Belgian troops at Liège, before securing passage home on August 8 aboard the Holland–America liner *Nieuw Amsterdam*, along with some two thousand other fleeing passengers. Recrossing the Channel, the ship navigated a minefield, was stopped by both French and British vessels and was fired upon. After picking up another two hundred stranded Americans in Plymouth, the *Nieuw Amsterdam* continued "a most strenuous voyage" to New York Harbor. While en route, it was fired upon again and stopped by the British cruiser *Essex* one day before finally reaching port on August 17 All in all, Hale wrote, it was a European trip "never to be forgotten."[4]

The outbreak of hostilities left hundreds of Hartford-area residents, like the Hale party, stranded across Europe. Back home, the news gripped the city. Bulletins posted outside downtown newspaper offices drew hundreds of onlookers, literally halting traffic. The savvy business-minded quickly took note. "The very latest war bulletins will be flashed on the screen between pictures," promised the Star Theater on Main Street in an advertisement on August 10 for its upcoming moving picture shows.[5] The disruptions to world trade and finance were felt immediately by some city manufacturers, like Hartford Rubber Works. Officials at Pratt & Whitney, Whitney Manufacturing, Cushman Chuck, Royal Typewriter and Underwood Typewriter and others expressed guarded optimism that any resulting material shortages and market closures would prove only temporary. Portending developments to come, Colt's Patent Firearms began receiving cables in early August from overseas buyers inquiring about delivery schedules should it become necessary to place orders.

The intense public interest showed that war was a big story, one that could impact jobs and livelihoods. But for tens of thousands of residents in and around Connecticut's capital who were born overseas or had parents who were, it meant more than that: it was hitting close to home.

HARTFORD IN 1914

Hartford County began the second decade of the twentieth century with a population of 250,182, or slightly fewer than one-quarter of Connecticut's 1.1 million residents. It was the second most populous of the state's eight counties, its residents largely concentrated in its manufacturing centers, as was true for much of the small, densely populated state. Hartford, the state's third-largest city, trailing New Haven and Bridgeport, numbered 98,915 residents in 1910. New Britain, already nationally recognized as the Hardware City, was fifth at 43,916. Among the twenty-nine municipalities in the county, only Bristol (13,502), Manchester (13,641), East Hartford (8,138) and Enfield (9,719) also had populations exceeding 5,000.

Hartford City's population in 1910 was overwhelming white—only 1.2 percent was classified by census takers as "Negro"—and of recent vintage. Two-thirds of its residents had either been born outside the United States or had one or both parents who were. More than 10,000 city residents were born in, or had both parents emigrate from, the Russian Empire, including Poles and Jewish refuges escaping czarist persecution. A total of 17,495 city residents were born or had both parents emigrate from Ireland; 7,256 had like connections to Italy. There were 5,249 residents born in Germany or to German parents in the city; more than 3,200 were born in Austria-Hungary or had parents who were native subjects of the Austro-Hungarian emperor. Foreign-born residents constituted 31.6 and 41.0 percent of the residents of Hartford and New Britain, respectively.

The pace of immigration-fueled growth, characteristic of the late nineteenth and early twentieth centuries, continued through the decade. By September 1915, the city's population was estimated at 138,132 residents, an astounding 28 percent increase in five years. By 1920, Hartford had become the nation's forty-sixth-largest city, with 138,036 residents. New Britain saw its population increase by 15,000 through the decade, and Hartford County as a whole added 86,000 residents.

The surge in non-Anglo immigration—a statewide phenomenon also evident in the largest counties, New Haven and Fairfield—dramatically changed Connecticut's social and demographic landscape and unsettled the ruling Yankee establishment. Small-town, moneyed interests had long held sway in the Republican-controlled Connecticut General Assembly. The constitution of 1818, which remained in force until 1965, guaranteed some of the state's smallest towns an equal number of representatives—two—as the largest cities, effectively disenfranchising the waves of city-dwelling,

		Hartford County	Hartford City	New Britain City
Population	1900	195,480	79,850	25,998
	1910	250,182	98.915	43,916
	1920	336,027	138,036	59,316
Percent Foreign Born	1900	27.9	29.6	35.7
	1910	31.7	31.6	41
	1920	28.8	29.5	35.8
Percent Native White with One or Both Parents Foreign Born	1900	32.1	33	38.4
	1910	34.3	35.2	38.8
	1920	38.9	38.2	35.8

Source: U.S. Bureau of the Census

non-English-speaking outsiders whose religious and cultural traditions and allegiances were very different from those of Protestant Anglo-Americans: "The tremendous influx of Southern European immigrants into Connecticut in the first decade of the century effectively dislocated an older way of life and caused great anxiety among Connecticut Yankees," one scholar observed.[6] That anxiety would manifest itself in actions taken by state and local officials as the United States drew closer to war and reached full flower during wartime in a vigorous campaign to "Americanize" immigrant communities

One of the nation's oldest cities, Hartford was founded on the west bank of the Connecticut River in 1636 by a group of Puritan colonists led by Thomas Hooker and became the state's sole capital in 1875. By 1914, it had achieved enviable prominence in manufacturing, commerce, banking and insurance. It was home to the nation's oldest continuously published newspaper, the *Hartford Courant*, which celebrated its 150th anniversary that October; the oldest public art museum, the Wadsworth Atheneum; the second-oldest public secondary school, Hartford Public High School; and the first public park, Bushnell Park, nestled beneath the ornate state capitol building. Hartford was "a place of greenery and wealth, one of the richest small cities in America…[It was] the city's architecturally rich downtown, home to a preponderance of insurance companies that gave Hartford its reputation as insurance capital of the world," observed a recent biographer of city native Katharine Hepburn, who, in 1914, was seven years old and lived on Hawthorne Street in a house once owned by former *Courant* editor in chief Charles Dudley Warner, Mark Twain's coauthor and friend.[7]

At the apex of the city wealth and power were families who could trace their ancestry through centuries of New England history. Hartford native John Pierpont "J.P." Morgan did not make his home in the city but maintained lifelong ties. Before his death in 1913, he had funded the Morgan Memorial wing of the Wadsworth Atheneum and is buried in Hartford's Cedar Hill Cemetery. Morgan's contemporary, Morgan G. Bulkeley, age seventy-six in August 1914, was in his thirty-fifth year as president of the Aetna Life Insurance Co. The company had been founded by his father, Eliphalet, in the 1850s, and Morgan Bulkeley succeeded in transforming the business into a heavyweight, multiline insurer while finding time to serve as four-term city mayor, Connecticut state governor, one-term U.S. senator and the first president of baseball's National League. A young, Yale-educated attorney, Charles A. Goodwin, whose father, the Reverend Francis Goodwin, was largely responsible for developing the city's systems of parks, had run unsuccessfully for governor in 1910 and sat on the boards of both Aetna and Connecticut General. Just thirty-seven when the European war broke out, he would be put in charge of conducting the state's manpower census in February 1917 and serve on the State Council of Defense. Another Yale man, Chicago native Richard M. Bissell, the president of Hartford Fire Insurance Co., carried a surname with deep roots in the Hartford area. He and his family resided and hosted social gatherings in the red-brick Gothic Revival home on Farmington Avenue built in 1874 for the Samuel Clemens family. Bissell would serve as wartime chairman of the State Council of Defense.

Hartford had matured architecturally in the early twentieth century, reflecting its growing prosperity and aesthetic sophistication. The period was known for Classical Revival and Beaux Arts design, and buildings from the era remain today among the city's most distinctive and well known: the Travelers Tower, constructed between 1906 and 1918; the Municipal Building (City Hall), opened in 1915; the State Library Memorial Hall and Supreme Court building, completed in 1910; the State Armory, built in 1909; and the Elks Lodge and Hartford Club buildings on Prospect Street, erected in 1903. The city's first skyscraper, the eleven-story Hartford-Aetna building, which, until its demolition in 1990, stood at the corner of Main Street and Asylum Avenue, was completed in 1912. The downtown buzzed with activity. The streets were noisy and congested by automobiles and electric trolleys, pushcarts and pedestrians. Gridlock was a regular occurrence. "The rapid growth of the City in population and industry, and the ever increasing number of automobiles which use our streets, has within a short time caused a marked changed in the degree of use to which these two streets are put," noted Hartford mayor Frank A. Hagarty about the central intersection at Main and Asylum.[8] Residents worked in the office buildings, flocked to the concert halls and the theaters and shopped at department stores with some of the most iconic names in the city's retail history: Brown, Thompson & Co. ("Connecticut's Biggest Department Store"); G. Fox & Co.; and Sage-Allen, which lined Main Street in a continuous brownstone and granite bazaar.

An acute citywide housing shortage in 1914 was felt strongly in burgeoning ethnic enclaves of Italian, Slavic, French Canadian and Polish workers in the Frog Hollow, Sheldon/Charter Oak and Parkville neighborhoods. The migration of African Americans from the South, which picked up steam during the century's second decade in response to agricultural labor shortages, added to the problem. On the city's East Side, in the vicinity of Front and Market Streets, grinding poverty, crime and alcoholism were dreary facts of life within the overcrowded tenements. In her 1917 report to the City Missionary Society, associate city missionary Mrs. N.W. Hankemeyer reported finding forty-one persons living in a single apartment and counted 132 saloons along the stretch of Main Street between the South Green and the New York, New Haven & Hartford Railroad Co. tunnel on Albany Avenue.

> *There were twenty-two rag and junk shops in the area for which old women and little children collected from everywhere. No social life existed in the overcrowded tenements. Apartments were filled with children, animals and smells. Fathers would come home after work to find their wives worn out with caring for children, cleaning and cooking. After the evening meal the fathers went to the saloons, the little children went to the streets, and the older boys and girls went to a movie show or cheap vaudeville. Immigrants to Hartford felt the strong family ties loosened under the slum conditions of the East Side.[9]*

One ethnic group, Irish Americans, who began settling in the Hartford area in significant numbers following the Great Famine of the 1840s, had achieved ascendency in city politics by 1914. Working largely through the Democratic Party, the Irish also emerged as major players in New Britain and Manchester. The fate of the Irish Home Rule in Parliament was followed locally with great interest that fateful summer. On July 12, the anniversary of the Battle of the Boyne, the *Courant* published a lengthy account of the escalating tensions between the armed militias of the two opposing camps: the Irish Nationalists and the Ulster Unionists.[10] Writer, world traveler and *Courant* business editor Bidwell would return to the island a few weeks later and find himself covering an even bigger story.

Another political movement with ties to the British Isles also generated intense interest in Hartford in the prewar period. The suffragette movement received extensive coverage in both the *Courant* and its rival, the *Hartford Times*. On May 2, 1914, the Connecticut Woman Suffrage Association, headquartered on Pratt Street, sponsored a parade, described as the largest gathering of women in the state's history, through the downtown streets. Association president Katharine Houghton Hepburn, young Kate's mother, told assembled listeners that "you must keep up your enthusiasm and cooperation so that the representatives of next year's General Assembly

A Connecticut Woman Suffrage Association (CWSA) parade in downtown Hartford, May 2, 1914. *Connecticut State Library.*

CWSA president Katharine Houghton Hepburn (front row, center) and members of the executive board. *Connecticut State Library.*

will know that the woman suffragists mean business and will not be put off any longer."[11] The suffragettes had momentum on their side but still faced substantial opposition, from the governor's office on down. They would not see their hopes realized until ratification of the Nineteenth Amendment in 1920. In the interim, Hartford women would play a significant role in helping the state and nation wage war.

THE FIRST MONTHS

The year 1914 saw savage fighting across Europe on multiple fronts. After slicing through Belgium into northern France, the German offensive, which was supposed to end the war quickly, was halted by the French and British at the Battle of the Marne. Each side then tried to outflank the other eastward toward the Channel, culminating with the First Battle of Ypres in October. By December, the lines of opposing trenches had formed, and the western front had become a grim reality. In the east, the czar's invasion of East Prussia was smashed by Hindenburg and Ludendorff at Tannenberg and Masurian

Lakes, and a series of great offensives and counteroffensives between the Russians and Austro-Hungarian armies caused enormous casualties without a decisive outcome.

With exquisite timing, Bidwell returned to Ireland aboard the Cunard liner *Carmania*, arriving in Cork on August 6, just two days after Britain declared war on Germany. On August 14, writing from Hotel Savoy in London, he described the popular mood—"a cool mixture of English phlegm and quiet enthusiasm"—and the business-as-usual attitude, which he contrasted with how he felt readers back home would be responding: "Flags are flying in many place. Yet a Hartford man thinks that, were 'the States' to be in war, Asylum street would fly more than the whole number you see along the Strand from Charing Cross to Fleet street."[12]

As it turned out, President Woodrow Wilson took care not to drag "the States" into the war and, on August 19, asked Congress for a declaration of neutrality. By then, realizing he had stumbled on the story of a lifetime, Bidwell had secured passage to France, stopping in Paris, before proceeding on to Boulogne and Flanders. He was determined to reach Lille, which had been declared an open city in anticipation of the oncoming Germans. After walking the last twenty-nine miles from Merville, Bidwell reached the half-deserted town a day before the Germans arrived. One of only two Americans on the scene, he spoke with several German soldiers, including one who briefly held him at bayonet point. After leaving the city, he was detained in Armentières as a suspected spy by a French reservist before being allowed to continue to Boulogne. The peripatetic correspondent returned to London, then went back to Paris and then back again to Britain before his return in October to Hartford, where he regaled local audiences with tales of his exploits.[13]

Well before Bidwell's return stateside, volunteers with the Hartford chapter of the American Red Cross had launched a drive to collect money, old clothing for bandages and hospital and medical supplies for European shipment. Sympathy for the plight of Belgium was felt immediately. Reports of civilian massacres by German troops inflamed local readers, as did the burning of the city of Louvain, where about a dozen Connecticut seminary students from the Hartford diocese were attending classes at the American College of the Immaculate Conception of the Blessed Virgin Mary, part of the famed University of Louvain. Leading Hartford families formed a local Belgian relief committee and sponsored a benefit concert at the Parsons Theater on October 26. Afterward, organizers led by Reverend Dr. William D. Mackenzie established the Belgian Relief Fund of Hartford to coordinate ongoing contributions. Benefits and donation drives picked up steam through the final weeks of the year. By mid-February 1915, the activities had reached a tipping point: a statewide Belgian relief association, formed in New Haven under the leadership of by then former Democratic governor Simeon E. Baldwin, was established, and a Connecticut shipload of supplies was planned, with towns and cities competing to raise the highest amount. Hartford took the lead, raising more than $17,000 before the ship sailed.

The deadly business of the European conflict was reflected in a venture undertaken jointly by Aetna Life Insurance Co., along with the Metropolitan Life Insurance Co. of New York, beginning in late 1914. The two companies began issuing life insurance policies to Canadian troops, with premiums paid for by local villages and towns, using mortality tables based on casualties from the Franco-Prussian War. Metropolitan charged its ordinary premium rate for most of the policies it issued the first year. As its vice-president, Haley Fiske, observed, without apparent irony, the company soon learned that "the old tables were by no means adequate."[14] In Aetna's case, the company charged a higher premium and relied on the still novel concept of group coverage. Ultimately, Aetna provided nearly $4 million in life insurance, covering 4,312 Canadian soldiers, and paid out $225,000 in death benefits. A large part of the total was paid to survivors of troops of the famed Princess Patricia's Canadian Light Infantry Regiment, which was decimated in the fighting in 1915.[15]

NEUTRALITY AND
PREPAREDNESS, 1915-16

I n the spring of 1915, forty-eight-year-old Theodate Pope was a respected, well-known figure in the Hartford progressive and suffragette movements. The only child of an Ohio industrialist, she had enjoyed a privileged upbringing and traveled widely, establishing a circle of friends and acquaintances that included brothers Henry and William James, artist Mary Cassatt and Theodore Roosevelt. She had designed a few private homes and the Westover School for girls in Middlebury, Connecticut, doggedly pursuing her passion for architecture and breaking down barriers in the male-dominated profession. Her first project, completed in 1901 with the assistance of the renowned New York City firm of McKim, Mead and White, was the Hill-Stead, the family estate on Main Street in the town of Farmington, ten miles from downtown Hartford, where her father, Alfred A. Pope, proudly displayed his collection of Impressionist paintings. Alfred Pope died in August 1913, and the Hill-Stead remained a place for community gatherings and graceful entertaining, although Pope would have disapproved of the tea his daughter hosted a few months after his death for militant British suffragette leader Emmeline Pankhurst.[16]

Architecture and politics were not Theodate Pope's only passions. An avid spiritualist, she had developed extensive contacts within the movement in the United States and in Great Britain. London was the headquarters of the Society for Psychical Research, which was committed to investigating and proving psychic phenomena, such as communicating with the spirits of the departed. Pope had befriended a young psychic researcher and academic, Dr. Edwin W. Friend, who, with his wife, Marjorie, a medium, lived in a cottage on the Hill-Stead grounds. Friend was invited to meet with society leaders, and Pope decided to make the trip with him. The two, accompanied by Pope's forty-year-old maid, Jessie Robinson, secured passage on the Cunard liner RMS *Lusitania* and left the port of New York shortly before 12:30 p.m. on May 1, 1915. There were 1,265 passengers and 694 crew members aboard.

A subject of controversy since its sinking, the *Lusitania* was considered by its owners and the British Admiralty to be too fast to be threatened by German U-boats. It had completed eight Atlantic crossings since the war broke out. Its enlarged cargo holds, as on previous eastbound voyages, were crammed with material and goods that the German government could rightfully claim were contraband. Manifests showed the ship carried 4,200 cases of small arms ammunition from the Remington Small Arms Co. in Bridgeport, $100,000 worth of hardware from North & Judd Manufacturing Co. of New Britain and 205 cases of oysters from the South Norwalk Oyster Co. of Connecticut.[17] Because the added cargo weight threw the ship out of kilter, Cunard had reduced fares in order to increase the number of passengers and add additional weight in the upper decks, making the crossing smoother.

The German embassy in Washington, D.C., had issued a warning on April 22 that it considered all British-flagged vessels as legitimate targets of war and that any passengers traveling on them did so at their own risk. Pope first learned of the threat while reading the *Sun* newspaper, just as the *Lusitania* left port. "I said to Mr. Friend, 'That means of course that they intend to get us,' though the name of the ship was not given," she wrote in a remarkable letter from Hotel de Crillon in Paris to her mother, Alma Pope, two months later.[18]

The first days of the voyage passed uneventfully. Pope kept mostly to herself "as I was very tired" and at one point had her stateroom changed because of a noisy family in the adjacent quarters. On the morning of the disaster, May 7, the fog had lifted, and Pope and Friend stood on the B deck, starboard side, gazing out over the Irish Sea, marveling at the blueness of the ocean and the dazzling, sunlit sky. "How could the officers ever see a periscope there?" she remarked. They then walked to the stern, just as the torpedo from *U-20* struck the liner's starboard side: "The sound was like that of an arrow entering the canvas and straw of a target, magnified a thousand times and I imagined I heard a dull explosion follow. The water and timbers flew past the deck. Mr. Friend struck his fist in his hand and said, 'By Jove, they've got us.'" Within seconds, the 786-foot-long vessel began listing heavily to starboard. The B deck

Lusitania survivor Theodate Pope in 1915. *Archives Hill-Stead Museum, Farmington, Connecticut.*

was crowded with panicked passengers, and the first lifeboat was lowered, its occupants spilling into the sea. The great ship was sinking rapidly. Reaching port side, as additional lifeboats were being lowered, Friend urged Pope to climb into one. "He would not take a place in one as long as there were still women aboard and, as I would not leave him, we pushed our way towards the stern, which was now uphill work, as the bow was sinking so rapidly." Finding three life belts, Friend tied them on to Pope, her maid and himself, and the three reached the ship's rail. Friend jumped first and then Pope—"I do not know whether Robinson followed me"—who found herself submerged, dashed against wooden decking and contemplating her own death, until surfacing a half minute later "surrounded and jostled by hundreds of frantic, screaming, shouting humans in this grey and watery inferno. The ship must have gone down."

After struggling with another clinging passenger, Pope lost consciousness. When she came to, she found herself on her back, gazing skyward, surrounded by floating passengers. The lifeboats were far away. She grabbed a floating oar and swung one leg over to help her maintain buoyancy, as her heavy clothing kept dragging her under. "I tried to lift my head a little to see for myself if there was not some aid coming. Then I sank back very relieved in my mind, for I decided it was too horrible to be true and that I was dreaming and again lost consciousness." Her next memory, more than seven hours later, was of a small, grated fire in the captain's cabin of the rescue ship *Julia*. She had been pulled from the water by crew members using boat hooks and, presumed lost, laid on the deck alongside the dead. Another passenger, Belle Naish, "touched me and says I felt like a sack of cement, I was so stiff with salt water. She was convinced I could be saved and induced two men to work over me, which they did for two hours, after cutting off my clothes with a carving knife hastily brought from the dining saloon." At the dock in Queenstown, Ireland, still suffering from hypothermia, she was carried off the ship, through the waiting throngs to a hotel, where she began a lengthy period of recovery and recuperation that took her first to Cork and then Dublin, London and France before returning home on August 1. One day before the first anniversary of the sinking, May 6, 1916, Pope married diplomat John W. Riddle on the grounds of her beloved Hill-Stead. Neither Friend nor Robinson was present at the ceremony. They were among the 123 Americans who lost their lives in the disaster. Of the 20 Connecticut residents believed to have been on board, based on passenger lists, 10 are thought to have perished. Residents of Hartford and Windsor were also among the dead.[19]

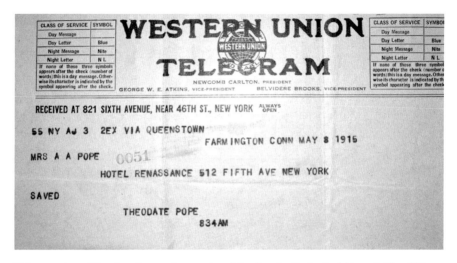

Telegram from Theodate Pope to her mother following the *Lusitania* sinking. *Archives Hill-Stead Museum, Farmington, Connecticut.*

Gas mask worn by Theodate Pope in London, 1915. *Archives Hill-Stead Museum, Farmington, Connecticut.*

The *Lusitania* sinking, following the accounts of German atrocities in Belgium, hardened the attitudes of many Americans toward the Kaiser and his government. In Hartford, newspaper readers soaked up accounts of Pope's harrowing tale of survival and the fates of the unfortunate Edwin Friend and other state victims. John H. Trumbull, the president of Trumbull Electric Co. in Plainville and a future governor of Connecticut, was so incensed by the loss of his brother Isaac that he vowed to convert his plant to arms and munitions manufacture to supply Germany's enemies.[20] Local insurers felt the sting of the disaster. Claims from the loss of life and cargo were projected at $750,000. The Travelers Insurance Company sustained the largest single loss in its history, with $422,000 in property losses and $22,000 in life insurance claims.[21] Local residents devoted to the cause of world peace reacted with utter dismay. The Connecticut Peace Society, a division of the American Peace Society formed in 1910, was an influential group of academics, clergy and civic leaders who promoted international peace and friendship and the use of arbitration to resolve disputes between nations and sponsored statewide high school essay contests to shape public opinion. At the society's May 12 meeting at Center Church House in Hartford, five days after the sinking, members unanimously adopted a resolution that "deplores and condemns those recent methods of warfare which have set at naught the established principals of international comity, violated all true valor and consecration of life to a just cause, and which have pointed the way backward to barbarism, all the more cruel for being more refined than that of the dark ages of the world." While lauding President Wilson's efforts "to promote a spirit of strict and impartial neutrality," the members asserted that they expected the president and cabinet "to determine what steps shall be taken to maintain the dignity and rights of the nation in this hour of supreme trial."[22] As events unfolded, it became clear that maintaining impartial neutrality and the dignity and rights of the nation were incompatible. Society leaders ultimately embraced Wilson's decision to go to war: "We believe the cause for which we fight is a righteous one, and that a just and stable peace can never be achieved until Prussian militarism and Hohenzollern autocracy have met with a decisive defeat."

The *Lusitania* sinking created a diplomatic and public relations crisis for Germany, but the U-boat campaign was allowed to continue, putting American lives at risk, until May 1916, when German naval and political leaders finally reined in the captains. Despite the danger, material shipments from North America to the Allies continued to expand, even as the foreign commerce of Germany and Austro-Hungary collapsed under the blockade, the loss of food imports weighing heavily on civilian populations. The disparity was not lost on German-American citizens and German nationals in the Hartford area. German immigration into the city dated back generations. The savvy Sam Colt had brought skilled German workers to work in his factory, providing them cottage-style housing in what became known as Potsdam Village. Germans contributed to the tide of post–Civil War immigration into Hartford County, built churches, formed benevolent and cultural societies and established social clubs. Among the best known in Hartford were the singing groups and choruses: Hartford Saengerbund, the oldest, established in 1858; Hartford Maennerchor, formed in 1884; Hartford Liederkrant, a German-Austrian singing group formed in 1911; and the Arbeiter Liedertafel. With the outbreak of war, civic leaders with ties to the Fatherland urged fellow residents to maintain an attitude of neutrality and even-handedness. At the forefront of that effort was the German-American Alliance of Hartford, a division of the Connecticut branch of the National German-American Alliance. Formed in 1906, five years after the national alliance, the German-American Alliance of Hartford comprised a dozen local clubs and organizations, including the singing groups and choruses, and numbered about 3,500 members. Its mission mirrored that of the national organization and various state affiliates: to preserve the German language and cultural traditions while opposing movements, like Prohibition, viewed as threatening. At a meeting on August 13, 1914, at Turnerbund Hall on Park Street, alliance delegates condemned what they termed "highly colored" initial press accounts—Belgium was not mentioned—and established a committee to aid the wounded of the German and Austrian armies, their widows and orphans.[23]

The conflicting loyalties of the German-American Alliance were demonstrated in February 1915 at a benefit concert for widows and orphans at the Parsons Theater. Two hundred members of the local singing societies entertained a packed house, along with prominent operatic soloists and a troupe of young female dancers performing a Hungarian folk dance. Flags of the United States and the colors of the German and Austro-Hungarian empires decorated the theater, and the evening ended with rousing renditions of the German army marching song *"Die Wacht Am Rein"* and "The Star-Spangled Banner."[24] Another benefit in April 1915 was held to mark the centennial of the birth of Otto von Bismarck, while a weeklong bazaar in January 1916 at the Park Casino, kicked off by Hartford mayor Joseph H. Lawler, drew thousands and raised between $8,000 and $10,000. In New Britain, a local chapter of Hilfsverein Deutscher Frauen (German Ladies Aid Society) was formed in

August 1916 to assist war orphans.[25] How much of the money raised from these and other efforts reached the intended recipients is impossible to know. Available evidence suggests that much of it did not. Testimony before a U.S. Senate committee in the spring of 1918 investigating whether to revoke the charter of the National German-American Alliance revealed that $800,000 raised by local and state affiliates ended up in the hands of the German government's chief propagandist in Washington. A leading promoter of the various Hartford benefits, someone well placed to get the "German side" of the story before the community, was Paul Stoeckel, owner and editor of *Connecticut Staats-Zeitung*. A naturalized citizen, Stoeckel was born in Berlin in 1871 and immigrated to the United States at age fourteen, settling in New Britain. He took a job at local German newspaper there, which he would eventually own and later merge with *Staats-Zeitung*. From his office on State Street, he became a leader in both the Hartford and Connecticut German-American Alliances; served as president of Hartford Turnerbund, a society of physical fitness devotees; and was active in the German Aid Society, assisting poor German and Austrian immigrants. In April 1916, he and other Hartford alliance leaders petitioned Congress to urge that everything possible be done to maintain peaceful relations with Germany, a prospect one unnamed member admitted at the time appeared "pretty dark."[26] Stoeckel's newspaper and his loyalties came under increased suspicion after the United States entered the war. Advertising and circulation at the *Staats-Zeitung* plummeted, and he was arrested in December 1917 for violating postal laws. Four months later, in April 1918, the German-American Alliance of Connecticut, following the lead of the national organization, voted to disband, and its remaining funds were distributed to charity.

The European war had become a truly global affair by 1916, encompassing nearly all of Europe, the Middle East, the Far East and Africa. The terrible toll exacted by the battlefields made the manpower needs of the belligerents increasingly acute. While U.S. neutrality prohibited the combatants from actively recruiting in this country, it did not stop young men from Hartford County, foreign nationals or American citizens from enlisting. Scottish-born David McPherson, twenty-two, quit his Hartford job as an elevator operator at Connecticut Mutual Life Insurance Co. and returned home to enlist in the British army in March 1916. Irish-born Robert Glenny, thirty-five, who had grown up in South Manchester, Connecticut, and served in Company G of the Connecticut National Guard, was working in South Africa when he enlisted with the British Expeditionary Force in late 1915. He was killed at Ypres in 1917. Michael M.M. Conroy, thirty-five, also

Irish born, was employed as a machinist at Colt's Firearms in 1915 and left for Montreal to enlist as a private with the Fifty-eighth Battalion of the Canadian Expeditionary Force. One of three brothers who served in the war, he obtained the rank of lance corporal and was killed by a sniper at Cambrai in September 1918. The first New Britain resident to die in the war, Sergeant William B. Denby, twenty-eight, joined the Canadian forces and succumbed to poisonous gas in November 1917. Herbert Worcester Smith from Wethersfield, Connecticut, enlisted in 1915 as a private in the Forty-eighth Highlanders, Fifteenth Battalion, First Canadian Infantry, and served in Flanders. After the United States entered the war, Smith transferred over to the American forces, attended aeronautic school and trained as a bomber pilot. Recognizing that up to sixteen thousand Americans like Conroy, Denby and Smith were serving in France and Belgium in their regiments, Canadian military officials formed an American Legion, although the name was officially avoided because of the neutrality law. When its first battalion, the Ninety-seventh, assembled in Toronto for deployment to Flanders in May 1916, ten Connecticut men were serving in the ranks.[27] Italy's entry into the war on the side of the Allies in May 1915 touched the lives of thousands in Hartford County. The Italian government took the position that it was not breaching U.S. neutrality laws by calling on naturalized "reservists" to return to defend the homeland. Heeding the call, about one hundred military-aged Italian immigrants from Thompsonville, the carpet-producing village in the town of Enfield, reported to the Italian consulate in Springfield, where they joined with fellow countrymen from Massachusetts and traveled to New York for passage to Europe in the late summer of 1915.[28]

Allied demands for manufactured products, consumer goods and foodstuffs jump-started the economy of Connecticut and the Hartford region. Manufacturing, which had been sluggish in the early part of 1914, rebounded and expanded. Total factory employment in the city of Hartford, which had stood at 21,066 employees in 1914, rose to 25,063 by 1916, about 20 percent of whom were women.[29] More than half the city's factories were producing products directly or indirectly related to the war by mid-1915. None benefitted more than Colt's Patent Firearms Manufacturing. By May 1915, Colt's had contracts with the Rumanian (as it was then spelled) government to supply 20,000 Model 1911 .45-caliber semiautomatic pistols, 40,000 magazines and 2.4 million cartridges. Great Britain's Ministry of Munitions was buying a minimum 400 Colt .45s per month. The Colt's Vickers Model of 1915 water-cooled, .30-caliber machine gun had entered production, supplanting the obsolete Colt

Automatic Gun Model 1895/1914 still in use by some Allied forces. In the fall of 1915, Colt's had reached an agreement, through the intercession of the British government, to produce 10,000 Vickers guns for the Russians, along with parts and accessories. The contract would prove problematic; repeated design changes and renegotiations stalled delivery up to the time of the Russian Revolution. The U.S. Army made its initial order for 125 Vickers in 1915, followed by 4,000 in 1916.[30] As a result of such productivity, the twelve-month period from June 1915 to June 1916 saw Colt's stock increase in value by 86 percent, from $443 to $825 a share. The company ended the period with $34 million worth of orders on hand and, flush with cash, ramped up dividends to shareholders.[31]

Like Colt's, Connecticut's other major munitions manufacturers—Remington Arms and Ammunition and Remington Union Metallic Cartridge Co. of Bridgeport, Winchester Repeating Arms and Marlin-Rockwell of New Haven—were boosted by foreign and U.S. government defense-related contracts. The inexhaustible demand for shell and cartridge cases and other brass products kept mills in Waterbury, the Naugatuck Valley and the Bristol area busy. Bristol Brass doubled its capital and saw its stock price increase by 35 percent in the twelve-month period ending in June 1916.[32] The loss of German-imported bearings created great demand for those produced at New Departure in Bristol, Fafnir Bearing in New Britain, Abbott Ball Co. of West Hartford and SKF Ball Bearings Co. in Hartford. The Allies bought military harness hardware from North & Judd, shrapnel-making machinery from New Britain Machine Co. and Union Manufacturing Co. and shrapnel shells from the Corbin Screw Corp. and P&F Corbin Co. divisions of American Hardware in New Britain. Leading Hartford manufacturers like American Machine Screw, Hartford Rubber Works and Pratt & Whitney, Underwood Typewriter and Royal Typewriter were in full production from Allied or domestic orders. The Jewell Belting Co. on Trumbull Street in Hartford, which continued operating one of its tanneries downtown, discharging into the Park River, had produced 300,000 leather bayonet scabbards for the British army and 1.25 million rifle slings for Russian troops by March 1917. Silk for cartridge bags and parachutes, was produced by the nation's leading silk producer, Cheney Brothers, at its sprawling complex in South Manchester. Glazier Manufacturing in South Glastonbury produced heavy woolen overcoats for British troops. The Ensign-Bickford Co., a world leader in the production of safety fuses and smokeless detonators, operated from plants in Simsbury and Avon in northwestern Hartford County. Company records showed it shipped hundreds of cases of its products to customers in

Russia; Canada; and its parent, Bickford, Smith & Co., in London, during 1915 and 1916.

With the bonds of culture, history, public opinion, business and finance tying the nation firmly to the Allies, influential Americans, led by former president Theodore Roosevelt and U.S. Army chief of staff Leonard Wood, were convinced that the United States could not remain on the sidelines forever. They organized, promoted and secured government backing for a camp in Plattsburgh, New York, to train officers America would need to lead a greatly expanded army. The opening of the camp in the summer of 1915 signaled the start of the Preparedness Movement: 1,200 well-to-do college students and businessmen, mostly from the Northeast, paid their own way for a month of bone-wearying drill, marksmanship, tactics, instruction in the use of machine guns and mortars and what one historian termed "a thorough indoctrination in Roosevelt-style nationalism."[33] About a half dozen Hartford students and a few Trinity College alumni attended the camp during its first season. Plattsburgh touched a national nerve—the camp was repeated in 1916 with additional camps opened in the West and Midwest. Trinity College veterans of the first camp publicly urged fellow alumni to participate—"Trinity has always been a leader in times of national stress and is expected to lead in 1916"[34]—and the Travelers and Phoenix Mutual insurance companies offered additional weeks of paid vacation to employees who signed up to participate. About fifty khaki-clad Hartford County civilians, part of a Connecticut contingent of four to five hundred, attended the 1916 Plattsburgh camp. In addition, students and young professors from Trinity and Hartford Theological Seminary began weekly Red Cross training at the State Armory, preparing for field service work in the event of a military call-up.

The wave of preparedness parades that swept across America during May and June 1916 reached Hartford on June 3. Ignoring a light rain, an estimated 100,000 spectators lined city streets to witness a two-hour, twenty-minute flag-waving spectacle that featured 17,000 marchers, led by the crew of the USS *Utah* and the Connecticut National Guard. Major employers like Colt's Firearms, Pratt & Whitney, Hartford Rubber Works and Travelers contributed 1,000 or more marchers each. Bankers and lawyers, factory workers and retail employees, postal carriers and firemen, ministers and female phone operators marched. So did Boy Scouts and Camp Fire Girls, Red Cross volunteers and military veterans and delegations from other towns and cities in Hartford County and throughout Connecticut. The lines of marchers passed the Main Street reviewing stand at the historic Old

State House, where Governor Marcus H. Holcomb and other dignitaries looked on. "Every citizen of Connecticut should feel as proud as I do of this splendid demonstration of the readiness of our citizens to support the principle of preparedness—not for war, but for the defense of homes, loved ones and American institutions. Hartford staged a wonderful spectacle…It was a real lesson in patriotism," Holcomb said.[35]

That same day, President Wilson signed the National Defense Act into law. It increased the size of the army and the National Guard, which became a true reserve, subject to overseas duty and service during periods of national emergency. Fifteen days later, on June 18, President Wilson used his newly created authority to call the state militias, including Connecticut's, to duty in the Southwest. The mission was to provide backup to the regular army, which was then pursuing Francisco "Pancho" Villa into northern Mexico. The bulk of Connecticut's National Guard, numbering then about 3,700 men, was mobilized, including its two historic infantry regiments; two troops of cavalry; one battalion and three batteries of field artillery, signal corps and ambulance companies, as well as a field hospital. Amid great public excitement, guardsmen of the First Infantry Regiment, composed of companies from Hartford, New Britain, Bristol, Manchester and the towns of Middletown, Willimantic and Winsted outside Hartford County, assembled at local armories, where they were ordered to Niantic for train transport to the Mexican border. Aetna Life president Morgan G. Bulkeley, who had two sons serving in Troop B, one of the guard's two cavalry units, personally paid for sixty horses to bring the mount-strapped, 100-member unit to full complement.[36] By early July, initial battalions of the First Infantry and the New Haven–based Second Infantry had made camp in Nogales, Arizona, beginning what became a three-month deployment. The officers and men saw no action but put up with searing heat, dust, violent thunderstorms, swarms of insects, poor food and shortages of water and supplies. The monotony of camp life was interrupted by long marches and maneuvers critiqued by regular army officers and a visit by Holcomb in late September. Recalled in October, the units were greeted warmly upon their return to Connecticut. While they had accomplished little, the guardsmen gained valuable experience in mobilization, drill, marksmanship and field training that they would soon put to use.

National Preparedness dominated the political landscape in the fall of 1916. Spending for the army and navy had dramatically increased, and the National Council of Defense was established. Frustrations with Mexico had continued and would soon culminate in February 1917 with publication

Connecticut guardsmen on mess duty along the Mexican border, 1916. *Connecticut State Library.*

of the notorious Zimmerman telegram. Still, the reelection of Woodrow Wilson, whose supporters campaigned that "He kept us out of war," reflected the national ambivalence over abandoning neutrality. Wilson's triumph over Republican candidate Charles Evans Hughes, however, failed to include Connecticut, a state the Democrat had taken four years before, assisted significantly by the Republican-Progressive split. With that fracture now healed, Hughes carried the Nutmeg State, and Holcomb, despite not actively campaigning, was reelected by more than twelve thousand votes.

Hartford Prepares for War, January 1917–April 6, 1917

S peaking to a luncheon audience in Hartford on March 21, 1917, Governor Marcus Hensey Holcomb lamented the state of American military readiness, calling it "dangerous and disgraceful" even as the dark clouds of war now threatened to burst. "It has been said that we are facing war. We have been in war for some time…We have been a party to war, but we have submitted to attacks upon our rights and have afforded no resistance. Congress has now been called for extra session, April 2. At that time it is probable there will be a declaration the nation is at war." The governor reminded his listeners that, mindful of the seriousness of the situation, he had authorized a census of all Connecticut males, age sixteen and older, and called for the creation of an armed, equipped home guard to combat the dark forces that he knew were actively working against the interests of the United States and the state of Connecticut: "Connecticut is in the most dangerous position of any state in the Union. You don't realize the condition—if you knew some of the things which have come to me you would be scared to death. I am. In the city of Hartford, drill is going on every night, and it is not in the interest of the United States. We needed a home guard, in my estimation."[37]

Over the next few days, Holcomb drove home the message: spies and saboteurs were searching for vulnerabilities in the state's industrial landscape, then responsible for producing 54 percent of the nation's arms and munitions. "It is up to us to be more cautious than folks in some other states have to be. It is up to us to see that plotters in Germany's interest do not put these big munitions plants out of business or attempt to delay their output."[38] The governor viewed the state's factories, with their largely alien, non-Anglo-American workforces as vulnerable to attack. The tensions and anxieties of recent weeks, stoked by rumors and incidents, real and imagined, had fed those suspicions, widely shared by many within and outside state government. That Holcomb had already begun steps to prepare the state for war, and protect it from the threat of enemies within, was indicative of the forceful leadership style he would demonstrate over the next two years.

Though not widely remembered today, Holcomb carries the distinction of serving as Connecticut's third war governor, following in the footsteps of Jonathan Trumbull in the American Revolution and William A. Buckingham during the Civil War. Born in 1844 on a farm in New Hartford in Litchfield County, Holcomb had enjoyed a long, distinguished career in law, banking and politics before serving as governor. While still a young attorney, he moved his practice to the Hartford County town of Southington, where he made his home, and in the following year, 1873, was elected judge of Probate, a position he held for thirty years. Originally a Democrat, he switched party affiliation in the 1880s. Highlights of his political résumé included election to the state senate in 1893, service as Hartford County treasurer from 1893 to 1910, delegate to the 1902 state Constitutional Convention and election as Speaker of the state House of Representatives in 1905. Two years later, in 1907, he was sworn in as state attorney general, a position he held until his elevation to the Superior Court bench in 1910. In September 1914, at the Republican State Convention in New Haven, against his stated wishes, he received his party's nod as its candidate for governor. He accepted the nomination but, as a sitting judge, refused to campaign and continued hearing cases even after his election. He finally stepped down from the bench on his seventieth birthday, November 28, 1914, having reached the judicial mandatory retirement age.

Holcomb began his second term on January 3, 1917. By then seventy-two years old, a widower since the death of his wife, Sarah Bennett Holcomb, in 1901, he maintained strong ties to his adopted hometown. He kept his home on Main Street, across from the town green, served as president of Southington Savings Bank and sat on the board of directors of several local corporations. A devout Baptist and member of the Masonic order, he possessed energy and decisiveness a much younger man would envy. His personal motto—"Honesty, Industry and Sobriety"[39]—reflected his deeply conservative character. He opposed women's suffrage and any changes to the state's Sunday blue laws. Although he had refused to campaign, he showed no reluctance to keep silent or equivocate on matters he felt strongly about, such as military preparedness or his contempt for the German government. Samples of writings from his official papers show a pen honed by decades of legal training, no-nonsense and to the point. Universal Film Co. president Carl Laemmle asked Holcomb in 1917 to add his New Year's wishes to a compilation Laemmle was compiling from public figures around the country that would be shown on movie screens and published in newspapers nationwide. Declining to select a greeting from Laemmle's proffered list, Holcomb offered his own instead: "We must wage this war until humanity is emancipated from autocratic domination." After a War Department functionary sent a telegram to Holcomb urging that he

Connecticut governor Marcus H. Holcomb. *Connecticut State Library.*

reconsider his refusal to sponsor a trip by a group of civilians to Camp Perry, Ohio, for small-arms training, he received an unambiguous brush-off:

All of our National Guard are overseas engaged in small and large arms practice, and from all accounts are proficient. We have 10,000 Home Guard armed and equipped, and all engaged in frequent small arms practice. The thousands of young men from this State who are constantly being sent to cantonments are there receiving instruction in small arms practice. In addition to all this, I fail to see the necessity of sending sixteen civilians to a camp for practice.

In June 1918, a YMCA recruiter asked for Holcomb's assessment of *Courant* reporter Daniel Bidwell, who had applied for a posting as an overseas field secretary. After describing Bidwell as "erratic" and prone to wanderlust, Holcomb concluded with a hint of wit: "He was a passenger on the Ford ship [Henry Ford's quixotic Peace Ship mission in 1915] and has been across two or three times I think since, and my acquaintance with these facts leads me to think that he might not be fitted to settle down to serious work which would not be of such a spectacular nature."[40]

On February 3, two days after the German Empire resumed its campaign of unrestricted submarine warfare against neutral shipping, President Wilson announced the United States was breaking off diplomatic relations with the Kaiser's government. Holcomb immediately offered support, the first state governor to do so: "You can depend upon the loyal support of Connecticut," read the telegram from the Republican governor. Three days later, on February 6, Holcomb addressed a joint session of the Connecticut General Assembly. In one of the most impactful speeches in state history, the governor told legislators that Connecticut—"the arsenal of the nation"—must ready itself "with feverish intensity" and mobilize all available resources for the impending conflict: "I recommend that power be given to your governor to take a census, classified with a view to their availability for the various activities of war, of the men of the state, together with an inventory of those physical resources of the state which war would call into requisition." Befitting his fiscal conservatism, Holcomb assured lawmakers that the enumeration could be undertaken at minimal expense using volunteers.[41] The House and senate endorsed the plan, and work began immediately. Hartford attorney Charles A. Goodwin, forty-one, whom Holcomb credited with coming up with the idea, led the group of eleven census assistants selected by Holcomb to oversee the counting of all state males, including aliens. Additional inventories were begun of the state's factories and farms, crops and livestock, doctors and nurses and automobiles.

The manpower census was completed with remarkable speed. Working from offices in the Connecticut Mutual Building on Pearl Street, with census blanks and punched cards prepared by clerical staff, commissions, identification badges and forms were sent out to canvassers in all 168 towns. By late February, the enumeration was well underway, and by the time war was declared on April 6, it was complete. A total of 502,979 names were compiled and categorized by occupation and skill set, prior military experience, age range and dependency and residency (citizen or alien) status. In Hartford, canvassers were appointed within individual factories, shops or places of business to survey co-workers. Political ward leaders, Republican and Democrat, worked the neighborhoods. In Bristol, Mayor Joseph F. Dutton proudly led groups of high school student volunteers into each factory where they distributed a total of six thousand census blanks. Shop foremen, assisted by interpreters, watched as the forms were filled out. The city's census commission chairman, Henry E. Cottle, reported on March 27 that canvassers had counted and processed 8,367 names, while spending just $79.11 on office supplies and fuel. Local census takers were clearly pleased with their efforts. In Bloomfield, Hartford's rural neighbor, census supervisor George F. Humphrey reported that his 14 fellow census commissioners overcame "bad traveling and sickness" to collect 752 names. Humphrey noted with satisfaction that some of those names had not previously appeared on the town's personal property tax rolls, an observation also made by Granby commission chief Eugene E. Goddard. In his report, Goddard said commissioners were often met with suspicion by local famers and farm laborers "feeling that to answer questions meant that they would be called upon for actual service at once. On the whole there was a general willingness to answer questions when the party understood the meaning." Wryly, he pointed to how surprised his commissioners were in finding "the number of men previously supposed to have sound bodies who suddenly discovered physical disabilities."[42]

On April 4, 1917, metal filing cabinets containing the military census records were transported under guard to their permanent home at the Connecticut State Library for use as events dictated. In an unsigned memo, state librarian George S. Godard later summarized what he believed were the principal benefits of the enumeration. It had aroused patriotism in every town and family and disclosed names of aliens "self-confessed, in our midst," including those working in state factories under government contract. It had revealed the identities of slackers and personal tax dodgers, "made men take a definite stand" and—rather ominously—"disclosed and emphasized" the large percentage of aliens in the state's population at large.[43]

The census was undertaken as Connecticut authorities were on edge, fearing disorder. Armed guards were posted in early February at the State Armory on Broad Street and at smaller armories across the state. A company of Connecticut National Guard Coast Artillery was called out to protect key bridges and river crossings along the shoreline, and guards were posted at railroad yards and facilities around New Haven. On the night of February 21, eight fires broke out in downtown New Britain within a two-hour time frame. At least seven of the fires were determined to have been intentionally set by igniting piles of rubbish in cellars, similar in origin to reports in January of a series of suspicious fires in Hartford. The New Britain fires damaged stores, businesses and a Jewish temple and fire companies from Hartford, Bristol, Plainville and Waterbury were called in to help put them out. New Britain mayor George W. Quigley asked for and received Holcomb's permission to call out the city's two National Guard companies to help city police protect local factories from

Military Census–Form No. 1

State of Connecticut.

By direction of an act of the Legislature of Connecticut, approved February 7th, 1917, I am required to procure certain information relative to the resources of the State. I therefore call upon you to answer the following questions.

MARCUS H. HOLCOMB,

Governor.

TOWN or CITY_____ DATE_____

FULL NAME_____

POST OFFICE ADDRESS_____

(Street and Number or Rural Free Delivery Number)

1. What is your present Trade, Occupation or Profession ?_____

2. Have you experience in any other Trade, Occupation or Profession ?_____

(State which.)

3. What is your Age ?_____ Height ?_____ Weight ?_____

4. Are you Married ? Single ? or Widower ?_____

5. How many persons are dependent on you for support ?_____

6. Are you a citizen of the United States ? _____

7. If not a citizen of the United States have you taken out your first papers ? _____

8. If not a citizen of the United States, what is your nationality ? _____

9. Have you ever done any Military or Naval Service in this or any other Country ?_____

Where ?_____ How Long ?_____ What Branch ?_____ Rank ?_____

10. Have you any serious physical disability ?_____ If so, name it._____

11. Can you do any of the following : Ride a horse ?_____ Handle a team ?_____ Drive an automobile ?_____

Ride a motorcycle ?_____ Understand telegraphy ?_____ Operate a wireless ?_____ Any experience with

a steam engine ?_____ Any experience with electrical machinery ?_____ Handle a boat, power or sail ?_____

Any experience in simple coastwise navigation ?_____ Any experience with High Speed Marine Gasoline

Engines ?_____ Are you a good swimmer ?_____

I hereby certify that I have personally interviewed the above mentioned person and that the answers to the questions enumerated are as he gave them to me.

Military Census Agent.

State of Connecticut military census form, February 1917. *Connecticut State Library.*

violence, as it was generally assumed the fires had been set to tie up public safety and divert attention to make easier "the carrying out of possible plots to blow up the factories, many of which are making war supplies."[44] In the following days, Manchester police announced changes in its police patrols to protect against disorder, and exterior lighting was increased at manufacturing plants in Bristol.

Embers from the fires had only just cooled when an impassioned General Assembly met on March 9 to consider legislation creating a home guard. The bill, crafted by Hartford attorney Benedict M. Holden, was approved unanimously by both houses, with members of the House of Representatives singing the national anthem during the vote. Holcomb immediately signed the law that created a three-member Military Emergency Board charged with establishing an armed constabulary to quell domestic disturbance whenever the Connecticut National Guard was unavailable. Boys and men ineligible for military service by age or other reason were to be recruited, trained and equipped. Enlistment was for two years, and recruits were to be paid during active service equivalent to that of state guardsmen.

New Britain mayor George W. Quigley, date unknown. *New Britain Public Library.*

Under the direction of Hartford Superior Court judge Lucien F. Burpee, the Military Emergency Board set up   headquarters at the Old State House and established a network of statewide recruitment stations. A stream of recruits poured in, from boys as young as sixteen and seventeen to seventy-two-year-old E. Newton Loveland, who signed his home guard enlistment at a meeting of the Wethersfield Business Men's Association, saying he was "glad to do this."[45] Following speeches by Holcomb and Holden, who had also been named to the Military Emergency Board, at a Southington rally on March 21, 126 men in the audience—the equivalent of more than a company—immediately signed up. Simsbury had a complete company organized and in uniform by early April, reputedly the first town in the region to do so. In Farmington, one local patriot organized a 70-member cavalry unit, along with horses and trucks for transport, to patrol local reservoirs. Recruitment in Hartford city was particularly strong. Former *Courant* managing editor Charles W. Burpee, Lucien's brother, headed the first group of 16 enlistees announced on March 13. Ten of the 16, like Charles Burpee, had prior military service with the state militia, the regular military or both; 2 others had served in the militias of other states. One enlistee, a Pratt & Whitney employee and native of Hungary, had served four years in the Austro-Hungarian army. By March 19, Captain Burpee was leading a company consisting of 108 men, ages sixteen to sixty-four, through its initial drill at the State Armory.

By early April, four city companies totaling more than three hundred men had been formed with Burpee, by then a colonel, commanding the home guard's First Regiment.

During the initial weeks, recruits drilled in civilian clothing without weapons while awaiting delivery of uniforms, coats, hats, rifles promised by the federal government and revolvers and machine guns ordered from Colt's. One scholar observed that, even without proper uniforms and weapons, the entire state had very much become an edgy, armed camp by April 2. "As Wilson spoke a vast array of Home Guard contingents, city guard units, manufacturers' militia and assorted town supernumeraries paced the state's bridges and public buildings uneasily awaiting the outbreak of alien violence."[46] Members of the Hartford Yacht Club organized patrols of the Connecticut River. Incidents, like the arrest in Bristol in late March of a suspected German spy who supposedly possessed a suitcase containing maps of Mexico and the United States and descriptive sketches of local factories and other materials, seemed to confirm the darkest suspicions. The rhetoric of the state's leaders, from Holcomb on down, did nothing to lighten the mood. Hartford Fire Insurance president and soon-to-be state Council of Defense chairman Richard M. Bissell warned that fires, explosions and insurrectionary mobs, not marching armies, were the enemy's weapons of choice: "The excitement caused by fire and explosion brings out a mob...The cunning hand to guide is only awaiting this development."[47] Lucien Burpee, speaking at the University Club, favored by Hartford elites, borrowed a page from the governor's script, warning: "I have found that there are now more or less organized forces in the state that have infernal anarchistic ideas which they would carry out. I know of one company in particular, not friendly to the country that has been practicing and drilling as a rifle club."[48] Not only was a fully functioning home guard critical to meet such threats, but its membership also provided authorities a true test of individual loyalty. As New Haven state's attorney Arnon A. Alling bluntly explained in a speech, "The Purposes of the Home Guard," before an audience of five hundred men and women in Cheshire: "He that is with us is with us and he that is not may be against us and the government. The formation of a home guard is a determined effort on the part of the government to find out who are its friends and

A home guard machine gun squad on duty in Bushnell Park, Hartford, 1917–18. *Connecticut State Library.*

where every man stands. The time has come for Americans to show their loyalty [and] for everyone to step forward and declare himself."[49]

Home guard enlistments eventually reached 20,000, with 10,000 armed and equipped on active duty, spread among six Connecticut regiments, before being halted. At its peak, the First Regiment numbered 3,500 men, with six companies within the city and others located in other cities and towns in Hartford County. There was also a machine gun company, a naval unit, a company of foreign or naturalized Italians and a company of colored home guardsmen, mirroring the experience of African Americans segregated in the Connecticut National Guard Separate Company. "By its drills and alertness it overawed the disaffected element which at times was gravely threatening, and it broke up a series of semi-public meetings of Socialists," concluded its commander, Colonel Burpee, in his voluminous three-volume history of Hartford County published in the 1920s.[50]

The Homefront,
April 1917–October 1918

A t 1:11 p.m. on April 6, 1917, President Wilson signed the congressional declaration placing the nation in a state of war with the German Empire. The moment was nearly anticlimactic, given the excitement and tensions that had gripped Hartford County in the preceding days and weeks. The state's two National Guard regiments, the Hartford-based First Infantry and the Second Infantry of New Haven, were called into federal service in late March for domestic security within a day of each other. Local home guard companies, most still lacking uniforms and weapons, drilled and marched frenetically. Red Cross organizers held local recruitment meetings. The day before, on April 5, employees of Corbin Screw in New Britain evidenced the popular mood by covering 1,500 factory windows with American flags. An editorial writer for the *Bristol Press*, no doubt reflecting sentiments shared by most readers, laid blame for the war squarely at the feet of those responsible for the *Lusitania* sinking two years before: "That fateful torpedo exploded the faith of the world in Prussian militarism and sounded the alarm to all the nations that a new danger threatened them all."[51] The *Hartford Times* splashed a bit of cold water on those thinking the war would bring merely a period of temporary inconvenience: "The blithe spirit in which many people seem inclined to accept this war as something which cannot seriously annoy many free-born Americans is likely to receive something of a damper, not only when the draft begins to make felt its operations, but when people, perhaps not subject to the draft, begin to pay the bills." The initial $3.5 billion congressional authorization, the *Times* warned, was "but a starter."[52] On April 7, units of the Connecticut Naval Militia were ordered to the Boston Navy Yard. State and city political and military leaders led by Governor Holcomb gathered at a rally outside Hartford City Hall to pledge "all our material and spiritual resources" toward the war effort. "We have assembled this afternoon to give voice to the patriotic spirit of the people of Hartford and to send assurance to those who in this time of crisis are charged with the destinies of the nation, that the spirit of loyalty, which filled the breasts of Hartford's people in 1776 and 1861 animate us in 1917," Mayor Frank A. Hagarty told 1,500 onlookers.[53] It could already be troublesome for anyone whose spirit was not so infused: a twenty-three-year-old Bristol man was sentenced to three months in jail, having shown the temerity the day before not to stand for the playing of the National Anthem at a local theater, instead remarking, "To hell with the flag."

It quickly became clear to those in power that the United States had entered the war completely unprepared to wage it. As Wesleyan University historian Richard Slotkin wrote:

> *The greatest industrial nation in the world would send its troops into action without any of the finished goods of war—trucks, tanks, artillery, machine guns airplanes. These would be supplied by the French and British, while America supplied raw materials—and raw recruits. In 1916 Congress had increased the authorized strength of [the] army and National Guard to 225,000 but Britain had lost that many men in a week's fighting along the Somme. An army of millions had to be created from scratch, with urgent speed.*[54]

U.S. Army brigadier general Clarence Ransom Edwards, commander of the Northeastern Department, stressed the magnitude of the task ahead at a prestigious dinner in June at the Hartford Club. Edwards, soon to be commander of the Twenty-sixth (Yankee) Division, told the audience of several hundred military officials and civilians that he believed the fighting would last at minimum three more years and that the United States would need to raise an army of five million or more, with up to two million coming from the draft. Organizing, equipping, training and transporting such a force, while at the same time keeping the Allies afloat materially and financially until it could be put to use, required an all-hands-on-deck commitment on the homefront.

Charged with coordinating the war effort in Connecticut was the State Council of Defense. Like its counterparts in other states, the Council of Defense was formed under a directive from secretary of war and national

Council of Defense chairman Newton D. Baker "to marshal, by whatever means every force, material and moral, which might be of service in winning the war." During its two-year existence, which ended in March 1919, the Council of Defense demonstrated an efficiency and effectiveness, some would argue zealousness, lacking in many of its peers. Using his emergency powers, Holcomb appointed the council's initial eleven members on April 26. The business and commercial interests of the state capital were well represented. Hartford Fire Insurance Co. president Richard M. Bissell was named chairman. Attorney Charles A. Goodwin, whose appointment recognized his work on the military census, sat on several corporate boards, including Aetna Life, Connecticut General and Phoenix State Bank. Howard A. Giddings, an army veteran and Connecticut National Guard brigade staffer, earned his living as supervisor of agencies for Travelers Insurance. Joseph W. Alsop of Avon, a major shade tobacco grower, had coordinated the agricultural and food supply inventories of the military census. A former Bull Moose returned to the Republican fold, Alsop emerged as a key player on the council when its expanding number of appointed committees soon outpaced the existing administrative machinery. An Executive Department under Alsop's leadership was created to bring about order. Working through it, the Council of Defense exerted control over nearly two dozen committees covering all aspects of the war effort. The larger, more important committees maintained separate offices and full-time staffs, functioning as state government departments. The council maintained a close working relationship, sharing personnel and office space, with administrators of key federal agencies like the U.S. Fuel Administration, U.S. Food Administration, U.S. Employment Service, Committee on Public Information (CIP) and National Council of Defense. In addition, the council provided guidance and support to the town committees and war bureaus responsible for the conduct of war-related activities within their communities. By war's end, twenty-eight war bureaus and two town committees were operating in Hartford Country. The head of the Hartford war bureau was the mayor, initially Republican Hagarty, followed by his Democratic successor, Richard J. Kinsella. In his first annual report to the Court of Common Council in May 1918, Kinsella made clear that wartime necessity trumped all other municipal needs:

> *Until this war is won, not one dollar of public money should be spent on any permanent improvement that can, without loss to the City or its people, be postponed. Hartford does not desire to compete with the United States for*

men, materials, or money. America's needs come first, and Hartford, true to every tradition of this City, will respect the obligations that we owe the nation and will abide by the desire of those in national authority.[55]

During the early months of war, eight county coordinating committees—Arthur L. Shipman headed the nine-member Hartford County Committee—were appointed to provide linkage between the Council of Defense and Connecticut's 168 towns. The structure proved unwieldy, and more often than not, the council dealt directly with local bureaus and committees.

Nearly half the twenty-three individuals—there were two resignations—who served on the Council of Defense during its lifetime were from the Hartford area. Four of eight gubernatorial appointments in July 1918 had particularly strong ties, including two of the first three female appointees. Frank D. Cheney of the Cheney Brothers silk mills in South Manchester had directed the industrial division of the military census in 1917, served as chairman of the council's Industrial Survey Committee and was a key go-between with the federal War Industries Board. William BroSmith, the general counsel for Travelers Insurance, had headed the committee in charge of Hartford's War Savings Stamp campaign. Mary T. Beach of West Hartford, who led the woman's committee of the Hartford War Bureau, chaired the critically important Woman's Division of the State Council. Fannie Briggs Houghton Bulkeley, wife of Morgan G. Bulkeley, was appointed by the Treasury Department to head the Connecticut Woman's Liberty Loan Committee. She was also a ranking member of the Woman's Division, which operated its own organizational network and committee structure.

Meeting the military's manpower needs occupied state leadership in the first weeks and months. The Selective Service Act of May 18, 1917, had authorized only the second draft in the nation's history and required all young men, ages twenty-one to thirty, to register on June 5. In the days leading up to registration, 153,000 notification cards prepared from names taken from the military census were sent out to the draft-eligible. The day went off largely without a hitch in Connecticut, with 160,000 men registered at town halls and designated sites. That number included 16,891 Hartford residents who reported to booths set up in the city's fourteen voting districts. The turnout exceeded prior estimates by about 1,000, and streetcars were used in one district to accommodate the overflow. One-third of city registrants were classified as aliens, including 96 from enemy nations, and 443 were classified as colored. Employees of some leading manufacturers like Pratt & Whitney and Terry Steam Turbine Co. arrived at the registration tables with letters from employers asking that they be excused from the draft because their work in war-related production was deemed essential.[56]

Through the summer, local boards met to classify and enumerate registrants, conduct physical examinations and consider claims for exemptions in advance of the initial call-up. Three of the state's forty-four exemption boards sat in Hartford, working in overcrowded offices in the Halls of Record building at the corner of Trumbull and Pearl Streets. Crowds of young men gathered outside or posed for photographs on the front steps in their best suits and hats. Two exemption boards met in New Britain while three others were responsible for the rest of Hartford County. Appeals from local determinations were heard by a five-member district board sitting in Hartford. From the outset, tensions arose between Connecticut authorities and the War Department Provost Marshal's Office over the state's draft quota, initially placed at 10,977 men, after National Guard and regular army enlistments were credited. U.S. senator Frank B. Brandegee joined his northern peers in support of a resolution decrying U.S. Census Bureau estimates used in apportioning state quotas, arguing that Connecticut's high number of draft-exempt aliens placed an unfair burden on its naturalized and native-born citizens. Following up official protests

Registering for the draft on June 5, 1917, at Main and Morgan Streets, Hartford. *Connecticut State Library.*

made to the War Department, Council of Defense chairman Bissell wrote to Provost Marshal E.H. Crowder complaining that the census number of 1,719,623 "grossly exaggerated" Connecticut's population by 400,000 residents. It also failed to take into consideration Connecticut's high number of aliens and was blind to the necessity of maintaining an adequate labor force in its factories, so critical to war production: "And may we not insist that justice to our state can be had only by means of a credit to be given when ensuing quotas are levied. This credit should equal the number in excess of Connecticut's fair allotment apportioned to this state under the recent draft. This excess we believe to be at least 4,000."[57] The pleadings failed to bring about an adjustment to the census figures, but Crowder mollified state officials by informing them that "friendly aliens" were eligible for enlistment and that the state would receive a credit in subsequent levees. Using a certainly inflated census estimate of 180,497, Hartford's initial draft contribution was set at 870 men. The quota for New Britain stood at 513 and 958 for the remainder of Hartford County. The initial group of 4,400 state draftees, including 348 Hartford residents, boarded trains on September 20, 1917, bound for basic training at Camp Devens in Ayer, Massachusetts. The excitement of the day was palpable: in New Britain, 30,000 turned out in the morning to send off the city's first 200 draftees. Factories halted production, stores closed and even the bars shut down; "in fact every activity in the city was at a standstill until the boys had left."[58]

The draft set into motion the creation of the national army. Army regulars and National Guard units were to be sent to France, in the words of Connecticut adjutant general George M. Cole, "to hold the fort until the new army can get over."[59] Bringing the state's militia units up to wartime strength presented its own challenges. During their initial weeks of guard duty, the First and Second Infantry regiments had seen their ranks depleted by discharges for those with dependents and those who, because of age or failure to meet physical requirements, were considered unfit for the task ahead. The flow of new recruits had failed to fill the void, and by mid-June, the two historic formations had fallen 1,300 men below the federally authorized strength of 4,116 officers and men. The Hartford-based First Infantry reported a shortfall of 800, much to the chagrin of its commander, Colonel Richard J. Goodman. At a meeting on June 19 at the state capitol in advance of "National Recruiting Week," called by President Wilson to spur enlistments, state and county officials discussed steps to improve guard recruitment, particularly as the units were scheduled to be called into federal military service in late July. "It would be to our everlasting discredit if this

Draftees outside the Halls of Record building, Pearl Street, Hartford. *Connecticut State Library.*

African American draftees on the steps of the Halls of Record, Pearl Street, Hartford. *Connecticut State Library.*

Draftees leaving Union Station for Camp Devens. *Connecticut State Library.*

First Regiment went into the federal service 800 short," Adjutant General Cole grumbled. To prevent such an occurrence, Connecticut launched its own recruitment push on the heels of the national drive. Recruiting stations were established in local armories, vacant storefronts, chamber of commerce offices and in military tents erected in village greens and parks. The publicity committee of the Council of Defense brought in speakers for local rallies and cars and trucks to transport potential enlistees directly to recruiting stations. Manufacturers were asked to lend support. Members of the home guard were instructed to locate potential recruits. Four street corner rallies at different locations in Hartford on the night of June 28 marked "the first really successful day of the campaign"[60] and brought in two hundred enlistment applications. Although only twelve of those met guard height and weight requirements, thirty-three were accepted by army recruiters. Ultimately, First Infantry enlistment did pick up, no doubt aided by the draft-eligible now facing conscription and the fact that the regiment's companies had begun very public drilling, parading and establishing camps in parks near the armories. By August 1, the First Infantry, by then encamped in New Haven with the Second Infantry, had grown to a more robust 1,808 officers and men.

As the state took initial steps to recruit young men to send overseas, the first liberty loan drive was launched in May and June to raise $2 billion for the war effort. Hartford, as a center of banking, insurance and manufacturing, was at the forefront, setting a pattern for the subsequent issues. Sales of the bonds, which matured in 30 years at 3.5 percent interest and were offered in denominations as low as $50, got off to a sluggish start, until stoked by a publicity campaign whose slogan, "A Liberty Bond in Every Hartford Home," reflected the organizers' goal of tapping all levels of society: brokers and professionals, schoolteachers and shopkeepers, factory workers and washerwomen. Major insurers and manufacturers took the lead. Fannie Bulkeley's Connecticut Woman's Liberty Loan Committee proved invaluable to the campaign's success. "We are in the greatest conflict the world has ever seen. We wish to show that the women of Connecticut are lovers of their country," said Bulkeley, who would soon be sending two sons to France.[61] Committee volunteers in Hartford under the direction of Marie Truesdale Bissell, wife of the Council of Defense chairman, staffed bond sales booths in the downtown department stores, their efforts aided by promotions like a cash-only day at Sage-Allen & Co., when shoppers were asked to forgo using credit, as was the norm, and bring in plenty of cash for reduced-priced store items and war bonds. Local Boy Scouts assisted with advertising and

Recruitment banners in downtown Hartford. *Connecticut State Library.*

subscriptions during the campaign's closing days. Stands decked out in red, white and blue were erected in front of the Old State House, and military bands and chorale groups serenaded bond buyers. Church bells rang and factory whistles sounded citywide to signal the end of the campaign on June 15. "Never in the history of the city has a financial movement had the publicity and popular interest which the loan campaign has excited," the *Courant* reported.[62] The final push brought total city subscriptions to $17.4 million, 43 percent of the $40 million state allotment and more than double the $8 million raised by the second-place finisher, Waterbury. Elsewhere in Hartford County, New Britain subscriptions reached $2.4 million; Bristol, $560,000; Manchester, $459,000; and totals for Southington, West Hartford, Farmington and Simsbury all exceeded $200,000.

The Council of Defense Committee of Publicity was established in May 1917 under the chairmanship of Rocky Hill resident and State Compensation commissioner George B. Chandler "to assist in shaping thought in directions which would promote the winning of the war."[63] Assisting with military

Women's groups, like the Polish Women Liberty Loan Committee, were instrumental in the success of Hartford liberty loan drives. *Connecticut State Library.*

Boy Scouts selling liberty bonds in downtown Hartford. *Connecticut State Library.*

recruitment and the sales of liberty bonds told only one part of the story. Through the committee, which was officially recognized as a department in July 1918, state leaders conveyed the message of what they believed the war was all about and coordinated the means to get that message across. The committee tapped prominent speakers for hundreds of public meetings and recruited war veterans—Canadian, British and American, often recovering from wounds—for appearances in parks and on street corners, in factories, at movie houses and in music theaters. It made sure that propaganda posters favored by the Council of Defense, such as the omnipresent "The Prussian Blot," were displayed prominently on more than one thousand war bulletin boards in Connecticut towns. Every avenue of communication was exploited. One division of the committee, under the direction of Reverend Morris Alling of Rocky Hill, worked with the war bureaus to ensure uniformity and consistency in the highly scripted Four Minute Men addresses in movie houses and theaters. A motion pictures division supplied government-approved war films to movie houses. The division of press cooperation, composed of representatives from the state's newspapers, ensured that editors and publishers received daily streams of federal- and state-approved publicity and war news.

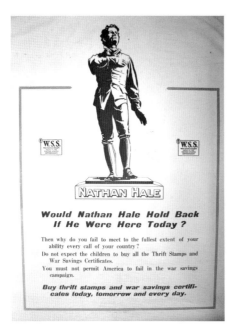

Would Nathan Hale Hold Back
If He Were Here Today ?

Then why do you fail to meet to the fullest extent of your
ability every call of your country ?
Do not expect the children to buy all the Thrift Stamps and
War Savings Certificates.
You must not permit America to fail in the war savings
campaign.

**Buy thrift stamps and war savings certifi-
cates today, tomorrow and every day.**

The image of Connecticut Revolutionary War hero Nathan Hale was used to market war savings stamps. *Simsbury Historical Society, Simsbury, Connecticut.*

The war rally became a particularly favored tool, beginning with the first, on October 17, 1917, which drew 1,500 people from across the state to Foot Guard Hall in Hartford. Co-sponsored by the Council of Defense and the chamber of commerce, the event kicked off Rally Week in support of the second liberty loan drive. For three hours, prominent speakers condemned the Prussian enemy, illustrating the message with lurid tales of alleged atrocities perpetrated by German troops in Poland and Belgium. Audience members were also treated to something new and different: a chorus of four hundred Hartford High School students performed patriotic songs, including one, "Three Cheers for Your Uncle Sam," written specifically for the occasion. So was born the Liberty Chorus, which became an immediate hit and a Hartford contribution to the national war effort. The Committee of Publicity began organizing similar singing groups in communities across Connecticut, believing, as the *Hartford Times* reported, "through music, especially chorus singing, a degree of patriotic expression can be attained that is impossible through any other medium"[64] Within three months, one hundred Liberty Choruses had been formed in towns, schools, churches, factories and stores. News of the success of the choruses spread to other states, and the National Council of Defense recommended their adoption nationwide. By December 1918, the Liberty Chorus division of the publicity department had sold forty thousand copies of its songbook and distributed 215,000 sheets of music. In addition to Hartford High School's, several Liberty Choruses had been formed and were performing in the city, in neighboring West Hartford and in fifteen other Hartford County communities.

The State Armory in Hartford was the site of a massive war rally on November 2, 1917. In what observers described as the largest gathering

A local soldier appearing at a Hartford war rally. *Connecticut State Library.*

Wartime propaganda posters fill a Sage-Allen storefront window on Main Street. *Connecticut State Library.*

held under a single roof in Connecticut history, fifteen thousand people crammed inside, and thousands more were turned away, to hear former president Theodore Roosevelt deliver a stemwinder about the war and what needed to be done to secure victory. Huge American flags hung from the rafters and draped over the galleries, and the Liberty Chorus, swollen to one thousand voices, performed. Roosevelt, who, accompanied by his wife, had arrived at Union Station just hours earlier from New York, did not disappoint his raucous, cheering listeners. TR praised the steps the Holcomb administration had taken, particularly the creation of the home guard, and his message clearly reflected the sentiments of his hosts. There could be no half measures. Everyone needed to do his or her part to win the war, whether at home or abroad: "We have two sets of enemies of this country. First, the Hun outside our gates, the Hun whom our people, our soldiers have gone abroad to fight; and then we have the Hun inside our gates, the disloyal man here…a wealthy man who tries to make an improper

THE WORLD CANNOT LIVE HALF SLAVE, HALF FREE

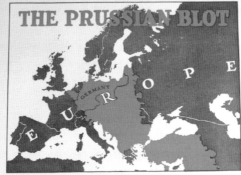

THE PRUSSIAN BLOT

100,000,000 PEOPLE ALREADY ENSLAVED BY GERMANY

President Wilson Says of the Germans:

"Their plan was to throw a broad belt of German military power and political control across the very center of Europe and beyond the Mediterranean Sea into the heart of Asia. They have actually carried the greater part of that amazing plan into execution."

THE KAISER PROCLAIMS:

"Woe and death unto those who oppose my will. Death to the infidel who denies my mission. Let all the enemies of the German nation perish. God demands their destruction."

WHILE GERMANY DREAMS OF DOMINATING THE WORLD BY FORCE THERE CAN BE NO PEACE

By Authority of the State Council of Defense

"The Prussian Blot," circa 1918, was a favorite of state authorities and displayed prominently on bulletin boards throughout Connecticut. *Watkinson Library, Trinity College, Hartford.*

Governor Holcomb and other dignitaries at the Liberty Cottage erected outside the Old State House, October 1917. *Connecticut State Library.*

profit out of the country, or an I.W.W. man or Germanized socialist who acts in the interests of the Hohenzollerns." No longer can America afford to be treated as "a polyglot boarding house" by "dollar-hunters of twenty different nationalities" who reserve "all their real loyalty for some land across the sea." No more can there be "fifty-fifty" citizens: "We have the blood of many of the Old World races in us. We are separated from all of them, and we will fail if we try to be like any of them. We must be Americans, nothing but Americans." Decrying German cruelty, the former president took aim at pacifists and slackers and urged listeners to do everything they could—pay taxes, buy liberty bonds, abide by food conservation rules and regulations, support the Red Cross and the YMCA—to support the boys in uniform. "We have gone in to save the liberty-loving peoples of mankind from cowering under the heel of an alien aggressor, and we shall not rest until we have humbled the pride of the most brutal, the most blood-thirsty, the most ruthless military autocracy the world has ever seen," he concluded in blood-curdling fashion.[65] "Colonel Roosevelt's speech was interesting and characteristic. Of course it went to extremes," observed the Democratic-leaning *Hartford Times*, which, unlike its Republican rival, the *Courant*, played its account of the rally on an inside page.[66]

The publicity committee's war rallies division, directed by Harrison B. Freeman of Hartford, coordinated five series of rallies between November and December 1917 and November 1918. Individual speakers were expected to follow a state-approved script, and reports were relayed back to Hartford after appearances to ensure that instruction was followed. During the initial series, which continued into early 1918 in Hartford County, a female speaker spoke first. She praised the role played by Allied women in the war and described how Connecticut women could do their part. A male speaker then developed the theme of how a dark German conspiracy had forced U.S. involvement and what dire consequences defeat would bring. The Victory War Rallies, held from mid-March to mid-May 1918, were designed to stiffen homefront morale during the great German spring offensive, when the Allies faced their greatest peril. The third campaign in June 1918 emphasized the need to buy thrift stamps and continue conservation efforts. Nearly one thousand rallies were held statewide during the first three campaigns. Less successful ones followed in July, August and November 1918. Connecticut was viewed by federal officials as a leader in developing the war rally strategy, and in May 1918, the National Council of Defense and the CIP sponsored a tour by Chandler through the western United States to explain his state's process and why it was working.

The rallies, the draft, the liberty loan campaigns, patriotic parades, fundraisers and outreach by the Red Cross, YMCA, YWCA, Jewish Welfare Board, Kiwanis and Knights of Columbus garnered headlines and held public attention.

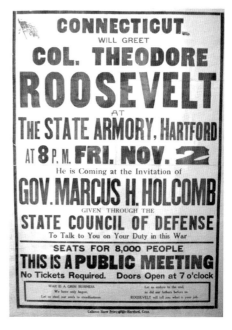

Poster advertising Theodore Roosevelt's appearance at a State Armory rally on November 2, 1917. *Museum of Connecticut History, Connecticut State Library.*

But nothing touched individual households during the war more closely than food. Hartford residents were expected to follow the direction of federal, state and local authorities and work to increase food production, preserve more of what was being produced and consume less, leaving more for the needs of the Allies, by forgoing meat or wheat on specified days of the week. On April 10, 1917, more than two weeks before naming the members of the Council of Defense, Governor Holcomb issued an emergency proclamation that created the Committee of Food Supply "to increase and conserve the agricultural resources of the state and with power to co-operate with other states and with the federal government, and to do all acts necessary to carry into effect the purposes for which this committee is established." Nine members of the committee—including key members Federal Food administrator Robert Scoville and his assistant, former New Britain state senator George M. Landers—were named, with Landers appointed chairman. Working from offices downtown on Pearl Street, the Food Supply Committee, which was brought under the purview of the Council of Defense in May, immediately launched efforts to ramp up production. There was a sense of crisis. Connecticut was a small state, heavily invested in manufacturing and dependent on imports from other states for 80 percent of its food supply. Given war demands, those imports were expected to shrink. Acreage needed to be expanded, and Connecticut Valley tobacco growers, represented on the Food Supply Committee by Alsop, pledged to convert their fields to the cultivation of beans, potatoes, vegetables, corn, buckwheat and other grains. A proclamation by Hartford mayor Hagarty read in all church pulpits in the city called on residents to plant home gardens. The board of parks commissioners voted to use part of the Goodwin Park municipal golf course for planting, and members of the private Hartford Golf Club agreed to plant potatoes on ten acres of club grounds.[67] Residents were urged to conserve as well as cultivate, and a one-day campaign to enlist Hartford housewives to pledge to do their part to abide by government-sanctioned conservation measures netted forty thousand signatures. Representatives of the extension services of Connecticut Agricultural College in Storrs— the future University of Connecticut—were called on to lend expertise in canning and food preservation techniques, gardening and horticulture and increasing livestock production.

Despite "splendid work" by home gardeners and farmers, results from 1917 disappointed those in charge—"not strenuous enough and not intelligent enough"—who looked for improvements in 1918.[68] One improvement discussed at a mass meeting of state farmers at the state capitol in March

Above: Hartford Red Cross girls helping with the war effort, 1918. *Connecticut State Library.*

Right: Connecticut housewives were encouraged to take the pledge to conserve food, July 1917. *Watkinson Library, Trinity College, Hartford.*

CONNECTICUT STATE COUNCIL OF DEFENSE

COMMITTEE
OF FOOD SUPPLY
36 Pearl St., Hartford, Conn.

HOUSEWIVES
JOIN THE ARMY OF SAVERS
SIGN THE FOLLOWING PLEDGE

"To the Food Administrator, Washington, D. C.

I am glad to join you in the service of food conservation for our nation and I hereby accept membership in the UNITED STATES FOOD ADMINISTRATION, pledging myself to carry out the directions and advice of the Food Administrator in the conduct of my household, in so far as my circumstances permit".

THIS IS SOMETHING YOU CAN DO TO HELP WIN THE WAR
ALL PLEDGES MUST BE IN BEFORE JULY 15th.
Cards can be obtained from your local Committee or other Women's Organizations

SIGN TO-DAY!
RETURN PLEDGES WHEN SIGNED TO FOOD ADMINISTRATOR, WASHINGTON, D. C.

1918 was to allow farmers, not government officials, to determine what crops needed to be planted. Pressure to expand potato cultivation the year before in anticipation of a market shortage that failed to materialize proved particularly embarrassing in New Britain. City officials had expanded potato cultivation on municipally owned farmland, only to find themselves stuck with bushels of unwanted, unneeded spuds. Mayor George W. Quigley, who had volunteered the use of his home for storage, found himself with a basement of rotting potatoes; as he later told the *New Britain Herald*: "After it was over and ever since, I haven't been able to look a potato in the eye."[69] A more successful campaign, begun in September 1917 and repeated in 1918, aimed at increasing poultry production and efficient egg laying by culling roosters and "slacker hens." Hartford County farm bureau officials and poultry experts from Connecticut Agricultural College visited demonstration farms to show owners how to spot unproductive layers, which were then slaughtered. "Every hen that does not lay except for a little while in the spring consumes more than she produces. Such a hen not only does nothing towards winning the war, but actually aids the enemy."[70] The Food Supply Committee, working in tandem with the Federal Food Administration, handled much of its own publicity. Promotional material—including posters, bulletins, recipes and other materials, printed not just in English, but also Italian, Polish and other languages—offered tips like using corn meal and rye, instead of wheat; eating fish instead of meat; and canning and preserving techniques for making jams and jellies. By September 1918, state officials reported that total acreage under cultivation in Connecticut had increased by 40 percent over the prior year. Wheat production, though still quite modest, had tripled; rye cultivation had expanded; and home gardens now numbered in the tens of thousands. Woman's Land Army volunteers, known as "farmerettes," assisted farmers in tilling their land. Tens of thousands of schoolboys and schoolgirls volunteered for the Connecticut Junior Agricultural Volunteers and the Junior Food Army to assist with food production, conservation and preservation.

Animosity and suspicion toward anything German—or the "Hun," as the enemy was frequently portrayed to the public—often reached extremes on the Hartford homefront. The right-wing National Security League director, Robert M. McElroy, met with Four Minute Men speakers at the state capitol, instructing them to depict the Prussian enemy as "vermin" and "vandals of the soul." Members of the Hartford chapter of the Daughters of the American Revolution called for the imposition of martial law to protect the country against "pacifists, spies, pro-Germans

Committee of Food Supply posters link potatoes and patriotism and urge poultry farmers to cull "slacker hens." *Watkinson Library, Trinity College, Hartford.*

and other traitors."[71] There was no turning the other cheek by Trinity College president Flavel S. Luther, who, speaking to fellow Protestant clergymen at a luncheon at the City Club, said: "When you pray, pray for the slaughter of the Germans, for complete and excellent victory...Forgive the Germans their sins? Yes, after they're dead."[72] Residents of the Hartford County town of Berlin debated for months on whether the name of their town, incorporated in 1785, should be changed. In Avon, a summer home with a scenic tower atop Talcott Mountain opened in 1914 by Hartford restaurateur and food-and-beverage magnate German-born Gilbert Heublein remained a focus of suspicious neighbors throughout the war despite the fact that its owner had offered its use to state authorities in March 1917. Rumors of stored munitions and wireless transmissions persisted, resulting in a top-to-bottom search of the premises in February 1918. The suspicions proved completely unfounded, but four months later, in June, Major General Lucien F. Burpee, commander of the Connecticut State Guard—the home guard moniker was changed in May—and chairman of the Committee of State Protection, suggested that Heublein "take steps" to prevent further suspicious illumination of the house and tower to allay fears of his nosy neighbors. A disgusted Heublein complied.[73] Perhaps more disturbing from today's perspective, letters were sent by state board of education secretary Charles D. Hine and state librarian George S. Godard in early 1918 to public libraries to be on the lookout for materials that could be construed as German propaganda or harmful to the Allied cause. A follow-up communication from the Council of Defense in July contained a list, five pages long, of titles recommended for removal from shelves. Included in the compilation were biographies of Frederick the Great, the Kaiser, Chancellor Bismarck, books on German history and travel and other works: "The fact that a book is listed here should not be taken in any way to impute disloyalty to the author, but merely to indicate the fact that material contained in it is not to the interest of the public during the period of the war, and should therefore be withdrawn temporarily from circulation."[74]

The Hartford branch of the People's Council of America for Democracy and the Terms of Peace, a national consortium of socialists, civil libertarians and pacifists formed in New York City in May 1917 in opposition to the war, was considered pro-German and eyed suspiciously by city, state and federal authorities. After branch leaders announced plans to hold a massed meeting, and local theater owners refused to provide a venue, the meeting was moved to Socialist Hall on Central Row downtown. There, on September 16, 1917, keynote speaker Anna Riley Hale vigorously denounced the war and the draft. Hartford police responded by breaking up the meeting, attended by about 250 persons, and arresting Hale. The message was received. By January 1918, the People's Council branch had ceased its activities. Local socialists—who fielded two tickets of party candidates in the 1918 spring Hartford municipal election—remained on the defensive and found themselves under increasing vigilance following the Bolshevik take-off in Russia. They were obliged to salute the American flag and offer public support to the third liberty bond drive during a comic-opera takeover of their headquarters in April 1918 by Colonel Burpee and members of the First Regiment of the home guard. "This change of heart was not voluntary," the *Courant* reported.[75]

What became known as Americanization—ensuring that its alien population remained not just loyal but also more tightly woven into the social fiber—became a major wartime initiative in Connecticut, beginning in July 1917 with the Council of Defense appointment of New Britain school superintendent Stanley H. Holmes to head the Committee on Foreign Born Population. Municipal Americanization boards backed by the chambers of commerce were formed in Hartford and New Britain. The stated goals of the twenty-five-member Hartford committee, headed by Mayor Hagarty, were "to take up the work of teaching foreigners the English language and to instill patriotism."[76] Under the energetic leadership of the committee's executive secretary, social worker Jane Robbins of Wethersfield, night classes in English-language instruction were begun in the city schools and soon spread into the factories. Hartford Public Library added reading materials to appeal to various ethnic and linguistic groups. "Be an American, one land, one tongue," read the slogan of a cottage opened in July 1918 in Pope Park in the heart of the city's factory district that served as a classroom and information center.[77] Americanization statewide was by then in full bloom. The Hartford-based Manufacturers' Association of Connecticut reminded its large, nonnative-born workforce to remain "100 percent loyal to America and its cause—first, last and all the time!" and to do everything possible (work a full day, save money, food and fuel, plant a home garden, report disloyalty) to ensure victory. The message, published in a widely circulated pamphlet in February 1918, was conveyed in English, Lithuanian, Polish, Russian, German and Italian.[78] In a move that reflected continued growth and expansion of its activities, the name of the Committee on Foreign Born Population was changed to the Americanization Committee, and on April 25, Governor Holcomb issued a proclamation banning the use of non-English instruction or administration in state public and private elementary schools, effective July 1, 1918. The Holcomb administration and the state's business leadership clearly viewed the transformation of Connecticut immigrant populations into loyal, English-speaking residents as a goal transcending wartime. A $10,000 appropriation funded the creation of the wartime Bureau of Americanization, which was provided a director and an office in the state capitol. By November 1918, the agency was coordinating the activities of dozens of Americanization committees, often organized by ethnicity, among forty-four local war bureaus and directing a campaign of speakers, posters and publications directed at arousing patriotism among Connecticut's nonnative born.

As the war in Europe entered its decisive stages in the spring and summer of 1918, productivity and patriotism reached their peaks. Factories in Hartford had entered full-throttle mode. All production at Colt's Patent Firearms was devoted to the war. The company produced the U.S. military's standard-issue sidearm, the .45-caliber Model 1911 pistol, as well as the Colt Vickers Model of 1915 machine gun and its successor, the Browning Model of 1917, designed by Colt's technical wizard, John M. Browning.

This liberty loan campaign poster targeting immigrants reflects Connecticut's vigorous Americanization efforts, 1918. *Litchfield Historical Society, Litchfield, Connecticut.*

By May 1918, Colt's workforce had swollen to almost 6,000, with women composing 10 percent of the workforce. At machine tool leader Pratt & Whitney, all 3,400 employees were working on war contracts, and the plant general manager complained that the shortage of skilled labor was limiting output: "If we could secure additional help of the requisite skill we could assist further. We cannot meet a tenth part of the demands made upon us."[79] Pratt produced the gauges and tools needed for the manufacture of weapons and shells to precise tolerances. At neighboring Hartford Machine Screw, brass and bronze components were machined and assembled into "21 second fuses" used in Allied artillery. The drop forges at the Billings & Spencer Co. turned out massive quantities of parts for guns, gun sights and mounts, shells, tripods, bayonets and engines. The production of munitions and parts for killing machines represented only part of the output. An estimated 274 million nails were manufactured at the Capewell Horse Nail Co. to re-shod army horses and mules. The Wiley-Bickford-Sweet Co. factory complex on Pliny Street produced 2.5 million articles to outfit the doughboys, such as canvas haversacks and packs, leggings and puttees. Terry Steam Turbine Co. on Windsor Street manufactured the turbines the navy needed to power torpedo boat destroyers and submarine chasers; SKF Ball Bearings on New Park Avenue was one of several radial and thrust bearing producers in Hartford County (radial and thrust bearings were essential for the operation of military vehicles and airplanes). Even Hartford's great typewriter manufacturers, Royal and Underwood, where women made up large portions of the workforce, were contributing to the war effort. Underwood alone produced 100,000 typewriters in 1918 for the U.S. and Allied governments: "When the army advanced the typewriters accompanied it," wrote the *Courant*.[80]

New Britain, like Hartford, became a major center for war production. A partial list of products manufactured at Stanley Works included valves for gas masks, parts for the shells fired from the famous French 75mm field gun, magazines for Browning machine guns, rifle and machine gun sockets and the hardware used for machine gun casings and to erect the stateside cantonments where doughboys trained: "It will be of interest to the Stanley Works' boys in the service to know The Stanley Works has played their part in fitting up the Government cantonments. All butts, bolts, hinges, etc. for all the U.S. Cantonments all over the Country are being furnished by this Company,"[81] the company reported. New Britain Machine Co. produced the only American-made antiaircraft gun of the war, 170 of them in all. Millions of hand grenades were produced at Vulcan Irons Works and at P.F. Corbin, which began producing war materiel in 1914 under a contract with the Russian government for adapter shells. By 1918, Corbin was manufacturing everything from trench mortar fuses and explosives to the hardware used in harness rigs and tents, belts and boats. American doughboys carried wicked-looking trench knives, ate out of mess kits and drank from canteens manufactured by Landers, Frary & Clark. Ball bearings, including those used in the British Mark VIII tank produced late in the war, were made at Fafnir Bearing Co. Underwear for the troops came from the American Hosiery Company and khaki shirts from Parker Shirt Co. In Bristol, more than half of the production of major employers like Bristol Brass Co. and New Departure was going toward the war effort by mid-1918, and smaller firms like Clayton Brothers Manufacturing Co. and Wallace Barnes did their part, producing surgical scissors for the War Department and springs for the Browning machine guns, respectively. In Glastonbury, long underwear manufactured at Glastonbury Knitting Mills and woolen overcoats from Glazier Manufacturing Co. helped the troops stay warm.

The contributions made by female factory workers to the nation's war effort during World War II, symbolized by the iconic Rosie the Riveter, have overshadowed those of a generation earlier. Military manpower demands in 1917–18 compelled munitions factories and metalworking and machine shops across Connecticut and in Hartford County to add women to their workforces, often for the first time. Total factory employment in Connecticut more than doubled between 1913 and 1918, from 169,677 to 355,994, with the number of women increasing 105 percent, 43,380 to 86,991. Patriotism and higher wages—although not as high as their male counterparts'—brought women from out of homes

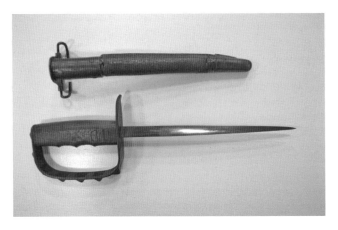

Trench knife produced by Landers, Frary & Clark, New Britain. *New Britain Industrial Museum.*

America's only designed and built antiaircraft gun, produced by New Britain Machine Co., on parade in the Hardware City, May 1918. *Glaeser Collection, New Britain Industrial Museum.*

Tank demonstration in Pope Park, Hartford, 1918. *Connecticut State Library.*

or working in traditional jobs in domestic service, offices or stores and into production plants. There, they handled myriad tasks traditionally performed by men: running drill presses; welding; operating cranes, screw machines and all manner of metalworking equipment; working in product design, drafting rooms and laboratories; doing warehouse work; and driving trucks. They put on khaki uniforms, gloves, rubber aprons and heavy shoes, as the jobs required. At the Maxim Silencer Co. in Hartford, female workers proudly showed their allegiance with a chevron: a red, white and blue shield, with *WWW* (Woman's War Workers) above and *USA* below. They overcame physical challenges without complaint: "There has always been a feeling against employment for women which involved physical strain, but it was considered quite unpatriotic this year to criticize any occupation. The number of standing-up jobs has increased and where stools had been provided for men they were hardly suitable for a woman," State Labor and Factory Inspection commissioner William S. Hyde said.[82] Working in munitions manufacture carried obvious risk, for women as well as men. Two young women were killed and four others injured on November 22, 1918, eleven days after the armistice, in an explosion at the Ensign-Bickford Co. in Simsbury while making fuses for hand grenades. To accommodate the influx of women, companies were forced to find ways to adapt, such as at Underwood Typewriter and the Cheney Brothers silk mills, where large daycare centers and nurseries were added.

Public displays of pomp and patriotism in Hartford kicked into high gear in 1918. Thousands of Polish patriots—men, women and children—paraded through city streets in April to show support for the war effort and the creation of an independent, democratic Poland. That was prelude to a larger, even more colorful parade on May 4, as an estimated twelve thousand marchers accompanied by floats and bands took to the streets of the capital city to celebrate the successful completion of the third liberty loan drive. The contributions of women, young and old, to the war effort were much in evidence. There were female liberty loan committees, the Visiting Nurse Association, the Red Cross, "Hello girls" in training to work telephone switchboards for the army in France, female factory workers, the Girls' Patriotic League and the Girl Scouts. "Soldiers in uniform, soldiers of insurance and soldiers of industry were in the three-mile long column, all honored and all an asset to the city, but mostly it was the women and girls who featured the day and caught and kept the fancy of the scores of thousands of onlookers along the line of parade,"

Women working at Colt's Patent Firearms Manufacturing Co. grind barrels for the Model 1911 .45-caliber semiautomatic. *Library of Congress.*

reported the *Courant.*[83] Two weeks later, on May 18, the Hartford chapter of the Red Cross launched its fundraising drive with another large parade, its ten thousand marchers reflecting the range of relief efforts being undertaken on behalf of the soldiers and Allies. Red Cross volunteers in New Britain held their own similar-sized parade the same day. The Fourth of July featured a Loyalty Parade in Hartford, with emphasis on the contributions of the foreign born. A weeklong state motor tour in September by the celebrated French Army Band, timed to coincide with the fourth liberty loan drive, featured receptions and luncheons in New Britain, Manchester, East Hartford and Hartford, where the members, all war veterans, were honored at the state capitol and performed on the capitol grounds and at Foot Guard Hall. The patriotic drumbeat continued into the fall at the fairgrounds, where war exhibits, sponsored by the Council of Defense, were featured attractions at the Connecticut Fair at Charter Oak Park in West Hartford, the Berlin Fair and in Enfield. Examples of locally produced weapons were displayed and machinists

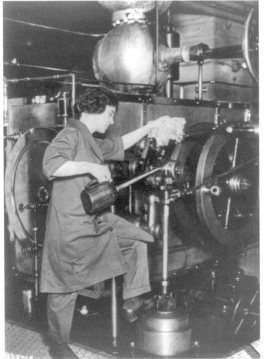

Above: Female employees at Colt's inspect pistol parts. *Library of Congress.*

Left: A female factory worker at Colt's oils machinery. *Library of Congress.*

A submarine float in a patriotic parade on Main Street in front of the Wadsworth Atheneum, 1918. *Connecticut State Library.*

One of the "Hello girls" trained in Hartford for switchboard duty in France. 1918. *Connecticut State Library.*

A Red Cross parade in New Britain, May 18, 1918. *Glaeser Collection, New Britain Industrial Museum.*

A large liberty loan rally outside Pratt & Whitney Co. on Capitol Avenue. *Connecticut State Library.*

demonstrated munitions making. Woman's Division booths highlighted war fashions and the diversity of war occupations for women. Results from the fourth liberty loan drive, the "Fighting Fourth," which concluded on October 19 with a rally outside city hall, highlighted the Hartford region's commitment to victory: $36.8 million, or two and a half times the quota assigned, had been pledged, and total subscriptions through the four wartime loan drives stood at nearly $100 million.

Hartford Doughboys in France

At 3:45 p.m. on February 5, 1918, in the vicinity of Soissons north of Paris, Battery A of the 101st Field Artillery Regiment, 51st Artillery Brigade, let loose a round at the German trenches. It was the first shot fired in anger in the war by men of the 26th Division. The Yankee Division, as it was known, was formed in July 1917 from National Guard units representing all five New England states. Commanded by Major General Clarence R. Edwards, the division had reached French soil that fall, the first fully formed American division to do so. Along with the 1st, 2nd and 42nd (Rainbow), the 26th would be among the U.S. Army's longest-serving divisions of the war and would sustain the fourth-highest number of casualties. Its story was very much a New England story, a Connecticut story and a Hartford story.

Two infantry brigades, the 51st and 52nd, each consisting of two regiments, formed the core of the division. One of those regiments, the 102nd of the 51st, combined Connecticut's two historic militia units, the New Haven–based Second Infantry plus 1,500 men from the First Infantry of Hartford, along with smaller contingents from Vermont and Massachusetts. Long-established Connecticut Guard companies with like designations—Company D from Bristol and Company D from New Haven, Company A from Hartford and Company A from Waterbury, for example—were combined. The merger left some 1st Infantry officers and men, including its commander, Colonel Richard J. Goodman, as excess, necessitating their transition to other units. Each infantry brigade in the division was assigned a machine gun battalion while a third machine gun battalion, the 101st, was attached to headquarters as a reserve. The 101st was composed largely of Connecticut Guard cavalrymen. The horsemen had learned when they reported to Niantic, Connecticut, for training that they would be toting machine guns not tending mounts: "I was glad to see the horses leave as I had never groomed a horse and didn't like what little I had of it," recalled Lawrence Bradford Neeld of Hartford in a letter to a friend decades later.[84] Neeld, then twenty-six, had finished studies at Wesleyan College and completed three months of officer training at Plattsburg before his assignment to Troop B, which became C Company of the 101st. Training at Niantic was perfunctory; the only guns provided were Colt .45s. In October, the battalion broke camp under cover of darkness and caught a train to Montreal. There, the men boarded a White Star liner that took them down the St. Lawrence to Halifax, where the ship joined a British escort convoy to Liverpool. After reaching port, they took a train to Southampton, crossed the Channel to LeHavre and, after three days traveling by train through the French countryside, reached division headquarters at Neufchâteau, where they hiked to billets outside the village: "We drilled in rain, walked in mud over our ankles and how we kept our health I'll never know," Neeld wrote. "We didn't receive our machine guns till a couple of weeks or so before starting for the front." Neeld was one of the lucky ones. Never wounded, he was hospitalized in October 1918 following exposure to phosgene gas but recovered well enough to be back on the front line by the armistice. Of trench life, he wrote: "Rats were prolific & cookies were a must, baths & delousing come only months apart."

The men of the Yankee Division received minimal training before reaching France. When the division arrived, its French allies schooled its men in weaponry and tactics and provided weapons like the Hotchkiss heavy machine gun and the universally despised Chauchat automatic rifle. Gas attacks, trench raids and enemy shelling in February and March during initial frontline duty along the Chemin-des-Dames ridge honed their survival skills. Reverend Charles E. Hesselgrave, the pastor of Center Congregational Church in Manchester, had volunteered as a YMCA field secretary and was assigned to bring oranges, candy, chocolate, toiletries and other canteen items to local men serving on the line. He described for newspaper readers back home what he found:

Our American soldiers are scattered in dug-outs and in caves which hold anywhere from 50 to 5,000 men, some of them a dozen, some of them 500; some of them 750. They are dug into this chalk-like stone, which

*is very easily chipped out, and held up with great props, beams, etc.
sometimes high, sometimes low; sometimes having several entrances, now
and then not more than one. The fields all about are full of shell-holes
and scarred with trenches and wire entanglements and all the debris and
destitute remnants of civilization and industry. There are factories torn
to pieces, sometimes only the foundations left. Hardly a house within
miles…has even half a roof.*[85]

When the desperate Allied high command needed combat-hardened troops to contain the great German spring offensive that began on March 21, the Yankee Division moved south of Verdun in relief of the First Division. There, in what was known as the Toul Sector, the first significant engagement fought by the division, indeed by the AEF, occurred on April 20. Following a terrific bombardment, 3,200 German storm troopers attacked the American line of defense near the ruined village of Seicheprey. The shelling left the largely untested Connecticut doughboys manning that part of the line dazed and confused, their telephone wires severed. They recovered in time to engage the enemy in vicious hand-to-hand combat within the main trench, in nearby woods and in Seicheprey itself. There, at first battalion headquarters, Major George J. Rau of Hartford formed a makeshift detachment of orderlies, runners, cooks and clerks to fight off the attackers. The Germans took significant casualties and fell back to their own lines early the next day, taking prisoners and captured equipment with them. American losses totaling 81 dead, 401 wounded or gassed and close to 200 captured or missing were felt keenly in Hartford County. Eight New Britain men were killed in action. Six of 73 Bristol men in Company D, 102nd Infantry, died; 18 were wounded; and nearly two dozen were captured. Another Bristol resident assigned to Company C was killed. It was the most devastating day in the small city's military history, with a loss of 8 men in all.

Company D private Lyman Michaels of Bristol was among the wounded. "I have a grenade wound on my head over my right eye and I wish you could see me with my head bandaged up. I know you will laugh it seems so funny but it's not serious and I am considered quite lucky," he wrote in a letter from his hospital bed to his sister three days later.[86] Corporal Charles T. Blanchard emerged unscathed but left with a piece of shrapnel that had pierced his pants leg without penetrating the skin as a memento. Blanchard's friend in Company D, Sergeant Erving A. Dresser, who had been fighting alongside Blanchard, was taken prisoner. "I only hope and pray that he will be treated as a prisoner in our hands would be," Blanchard wrote to Dresser's family.[87]

Sketches of trench life by Private Robert L. O'Connell of Southington, First Engineers, First Division, December 1917. *Memorial Military Museum, Bristol, Connecticut.*

His hopes proved well founded: Dresser survived the rest of the war rather comfortably in a German POW camp. The family of Private William O'Sullivan was notified by the War Department that he was one of the Company D men killed in action. After a funeral mass, the family learned the notification had been in error and that O'Sullivan was taken prisoner. He was repatriated following the armistice. Prominent among the dead at Seicheprey was Captain Arthur F. Locke, thirty-eight. A Vermont native, Locke had moved to Hartford in 1901, was married and spent sixteen years serving in the Connecticut National Guard. He commanded Company M and died heroically, refusing to surrender after being cut off from his men. "He managed to get three revolver clips of cartridge home, one after the other, in the faces of the Boches before they dared to rush him; he was reloading for the fourth time when they closed in and killed him."[88] Locke was the first Connecticut officer killed in the war. He is buried in St. Mihiel American Cemetery.

In late May, German forces launched their third major push of the spring. Breaking through along the Aisne River between Soissons and Rheims, the Kaiser's divisions reached the Marne, threatening Paris. Two American

The Fight at Seicheprey by John D. Whiting, 1927. *Joseph Brunjes/West Haven (Connecticut) Veterans Museum.*

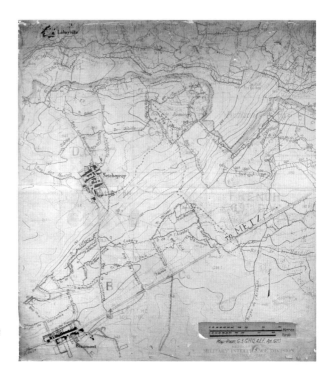

AEF after-action map of Seicheprey, 1920. *Joseph Brunjes/West Haven (Connecticut) Veterans Museum.*

Sergeant Lyman Michaels of Bristol, wounded at Seicheprey, is pictured here (back row, center) with other members of Company D, 102nd Infantry, at the war's end. *Memorial Military Museum, Bristol, Connecticut.*

Captain Arthur F. Locke of Hartford, Company M, 102ⁿᵈ Infantry Regiment, 26ᵗʰ Division, killed in action at Seicheprey. *Connecticut State Library.*

regular divisions, the Second and Third, were rushed in to help stem the tide, and in Belleau Wood at Château-Thierry, the Fifth and Sixth Marine Regiments assigned to the Second Division fought one of the corps' most iconic battles. Commanding the Seventy-eighth Company, Sixth Marines, was twenty-three-year-old Second Lieutenant Henry Leslie Eddy, a New Britain native who had clerked at Corbin Screw before the war. He was killed in action on June 4, the first officer from New Britain to die in combat, and was posthumously awarded the Distinguished Service Cross. Two days later, on June 6, Second Lieutenant Caldwell Colt Robinson of Hartford, Eighty-second Company, Sixth Marines, died leading a charge on an enemy machine gun position. A member of his platoon later told the *Courant* that the twenty-one-year-old Robinson, armed with a French rifle and a Colt .45 in each hand, had yelled, "Follow me, boys!" to his men and then raced on ahead, blazing away with his brace of pistols before being riddled by machine gun fire.[89] Whether the marine, himself wounded in the firefight, had embellished the story for the Hartford audience is unknown. The gallant young Robinson was the son of former Colt's Patent Firearms president Colonel Charles Leonard Frost Robinson and his wife, Elizabeth Hart Jarvis Beach, niece of Samuel Colt's widow, Elizabeth Jarvis Colt. Decorated posthumously with the Distinguished Service Cross and the Navy Cross, Robinson is buried in the Aisne-Marne American Cemetery. The Veterans of Foreign Wars Post 254 was named in his honor.

Ferocious fighting in the Aisne-Marne region continued into July. The fifth and final German drive was stopped at the Second Battle of the Marne. A massive French-led counterattack, involving eight American divisions, began on July 18 to reduce the salient, or bulge in front, created by the German offensive. A great but costly victory followed. Over eight days (July 18–25),

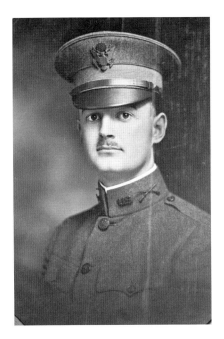

Left: Second Lieutenant Henry Leslie Eddy of New Britain, Seventy-eighth Company, Sixth Marine Regiment, killed in action at Belleau Wood. *Connecticut State Library.*

Right: Second Lieutenant Caldwell Colt Robinson of Hartford, Eighty-second Company, Sixth Marine Regiment, killed in action at Belleau Wood. *Connecticut State Library.*

the Yankee Division alone suffered 3,500 casualties, including nearly 500 killed, as its infantry regiments, supported by machine gun and engineering battalions, charged through picturesque fields of ripening wheat into the teeth of enemy artillery and demonically placed machine guns. Sergeant Howard R. Lamont of Meriden described to a cousin what it was like for Company I, 102nd Infantry, on the morning of July 22, the day his friend Mechanic Horace J. Tanguay of the Thompsonville section of Enfield was killed:

> *We had to take a large woods filled with machine guns. We took our formations and went over after them. Horace never knew what hit him. He was shot between the eyes. He was my good friend. I was buried for almost five minutes…gained my place, was burned and scratched by bullets. One went through my trousers' leg, one through my left sleeve, one scorched the tip of my nose. I had a dent from a piece of shrapnel in my helmet. Our company had quite a few casualties. Only seventy-four answered roll call that night.*[90]

Captain Daniel W. Strickland of New Haven led Company D that day in its attack on the hamlet of Trugny, outside Château-Thierry. In his postwar history of the regiment, he described how new, untrained men made a bad situation worse, ignoring orders and firing through their own ranks, increasing casualties. "It developed that morning that the last batch of replacements sent up could not even load a rifle, much less fire it. These men had been sent to the two companies, 'B' and 'D' in the woods just before the great advance and had only landed in France on July fourth!"[91] On the following day, July 23, four Hartford residents, members of Company A, 102nd Infantry—Sergeant John West, twenty; Corporal Francis H. Healy, twenty-eight; Private Sebastino Barber, twenty-two; and fellow Italian-born Front Street resident Private Antonio D'Ambrosio, nineteen—were killed in action in an assault upon Epieds from the Bois de Breteuil. D'Ambrosio left three brothers fighting in the Italian army and another with the U.S. Army. The Company A casualty list would continue to lengthen over the ensuing days. Sergeant Herbert Ratenburg of Manchester, a medic with the Sanitary Detachment assigned to Company B of the motorized 101st Machine Gun Battalion, had been in the vanguard of the Epieds attack. "It was here we got into trouble. Just imagine a vast number of troops advancing through an open wheat field with no protection whatsoever; advancing toward some woods after passing through this opening under heavy shell fire, to be met with machine gun fire from snipers who were concealed in the woods. These snipers did considerable damage," he wrote in a letter to a co-worker at Aetna Life Insurance Co. from the base hospital. Despite being wounded and gassed, Ratenburg had continued tending to the wounded under heavy fire and received the Distinguished Service Cross. He reflected, "It is hard telling when the war will be over but to be frank I wish it was tomorrow as I have seen all the war I care to see."[92] Connecticut doughboys professed nothing but hatred for German machine gunners, the cause of so much misery. Writing to his aunt, New London resident Robert D. Burrows of Company G, 102nd, wrote: "We captured a machine gunner and he said, 'Kamerad,' but a revolver bullet finished him. We never take a machine gunner prisoner. If you saw the American dead, which I have, you would know why."[93] On the final day of the push, July 25, an artillery round struck the tent occupied by Major Rau, killing him instantly. The highest-ranking officer from Hartford to die in the war, Rau, thirty-six, was born in German-occupied Lorraine and came to the United States as a small child, growing up at his parents' home in East Hartford. He had spent half his life in the military, beginning in 1900 with his enlistment with the U.S. 7th Cavalry and

Memorial poster to Major George J. Rau of Hartford, 102nd Infantry Regiment, 26th Division, killed in action at Château Thierry. *American Legion Rau-Locke Post 8, Hartford.*

continuing, following his discharge and return to civilian life, with the state militia. He rose through the noncommissioned and commissioned ranks of the 1st Infantry, impressing all who served with him, and was married, the father of a young daughter, when the United States entered the war. In August 1917, he was given command of the 1st Battalion, Companies I, K, L and M. One month before his death, a shell had burst near him, killing one man and wounding two others. "I'm going to get a rabbit's foot to wear. I'm getting tired of these close-ups," he wrote to his wife.[94] Rau, who was decorated with the Croix de Guerre for his actions at Seicheprey, is buried in the Oise-Aisne American Cemetery.

A twenty-eight-year-old Hartford nurse, Ruth Hovey, left a riveting account of her experiences at a frontline hospital that July. Hovey was working at Hartford Hospital and living at her parents' home on Prospect Avenue in April 1917 when she enlisted with the Army Medical Corps at Presbyterian Hospital of New York, where she had attended nursing school. She was sent to Europe and spent a year at a base hospital in France attached to the British Expeditionary Force. In June 1918, having transferred to the AEF, Hovey was assigned to Mobile Hospital No. 2 with the Forty-second (Rainbow) Division. Late on July 14, Bastille Day, her unit was camped at Bussy-le-Château, and the nurses had completed their shifts and turned in for the night. What happened next, as Hovey described in a letter to her mother, became a real-life episode of *M*A*S*H*. At midnight, a German shell flew over the nurses' hut and crashed in the tomato patch behind, jarring everyone awake. Grabbing their gas masks and helmets—Hovey said she alone was able pull on her clothing—the nurses rushed to the safety of a large, steel-enforced dugout. There they waited until the wounded began arriving, when they left the safety of the dugout to begin their work:

> *We operated all night under shell fire until about 5 A.M. when the shells began to drop into the hospital. Before Mary and I left the operating room a shell whizzed by and took a piece off the roof over our heads. Our sleeping quarters and two of the wards and the men's huts were wrecked. Two patients were killed in bed and others wounded, and through it all mother, everybody stuck to their posts and nobody lost their heads for a moment.*
>
> *Violetta left her ward for the dugout just two minutes before a shell burst in her bunk. A big piece of shell came through a window right beside the surgeon who was giving a transfusion and landed six inches from him. The marvelous part is, there was not a single member of the unit scratched.*

We vacated the position in the morning and a few hours later the place was shelled again and practically ruined. The Huns had our range exactly and there is not a doubt they intended to do as much harm as possible in spite of the four huge red crosses we had on our grounds.

Their hospital destroyed, Hovey and her surgical team spent the next three days working night and day at another hospital. "If I had time to think, the sight of our boys shot to pieces and dying on all sides before anything could be done for them, would simply have broken my heart, we simply had no time to think. We worked mechanically like machines while the rush lasted." When the lull finally came, the nurses rejoined their old unit just in time for another move. As a sop to her mother's anxieties, she added: "You shouldn't worry about me, for we have learned by our experiences that it is not practical to be so near the firing line." Hovey continued her service until her discharge in March 1919. She returned to Hartford and married Dr. Benjamin R. Allison in June. Two months later, Ruth Hovey Allison was decorated with the Croix de Guerre with a bronze star for heroism during her four days under fire.[95]

By late summer, fighting on the western front had tilted irreversibly in the Allies' favor. The AEF continued to grow in strength and power as new national army divisions and a steady stream of replacements provided by the draft began arriving in France in great numbers, more than 300,000 in July alone. Among those who were helping the doughboys reach their destination safely was eighteen-year-old Seaman Frank Kenneth Young of Hartford. Young served aboard the destroyer USS *Wadsworth*, which patrolled French coastal waters on the lookout for U-boats and helped escort troop convoys safely into Brest Harbor. He described his fellow crew mates as "always alert, watchful, obedient and brave" and spoke fondly of his wartime experience following

Decorated U.S. Army nurse Ruth Hovey. *Connecticut State Library.*

his discharge in July 1921.[96] Another navy man, Signalman First Class Lloyd Rogers Mill Linton of New Britain, also served on a troop transport until his assignment in August to one of the nation's mightiest battleships, the USS *Wyoming*, which patrolled the North Sea with the British fleet. A collision on October 14 with a German U-boat—a "tussle" in Linton's words—sent the submarine to the bottom of the ocean but badly damaged the *Wyoming*'s prop. Repairs were completed in time for Linton, a clerk at Stanley Rule and Level Co., to be present at Scapa Flow, where the German High Seas Fleet was interred after the war. While Hartford-area sailors avoided the lice, poison gas and deafening bombardments of trench life, they faced their own perils. Seaman Alexander Sandberg and Seaman Walter Rosensweig, both of New Britain, barely survived the sinking of the armored cruiser USS *San Diego*, which struck a German mine on July 19, 1918, off the Atlantic coast while on escort duty. Others were not so fortunate. Fireman Second Class James T. Halford, who worked at Royal Typewriter before the war, was aboard the transport USS *Mount Vernon* bound for Brest when the vessel was struck by a German torpedo on September 5. He was among three dozen of the ship's crew members to die in the attack. Months before, in March 1918, Machinist Mate Henry F. Lobmeyer of East Hartford was aboard the USS *Manley* when the destroyer collided with a British cruiser, causing its depth charges to detonate, killing Lobmeyer and several of the crew.

Army doughboys and navy seamen shared one common hazard. Sickness and disease spared no service, recognized no national boundary and favored no side in the conflict. Overcrowded camps and ports, lack of sanitation and the vagaries of the food supply, fatigue and constant stress—such conditions were ripe for the spread of infectious diseases like measles, pneumonia and, by the summer of 1918, a particularly deadly strain of influenza. One of history's greatest killers, the misnamed Spanish influenza, likely originated in the U.S. Army cantonments. Cases began appearing in France in April, leveled off for a period and then reappeared with a vengeance by late summer. In his history of the 102nd Regiment, Strickland noted that influenza and the pneumonia and colds that often accompanied it were a significant factor, along with mental and physical exhaustion, in the weakened condition of his and other frontline regiments late in the war. One eyewitness to the flu's devastating effects on American troops was Dorothy Cheney, a member of the Cheney Brothers silk family of Manchester. Cheney and her twin sister, Marjory ("Peg"), had arrived in Paris in the fall of 1917 to assist displaced children and had gone to work at the Red Cross office in the city. In May 1918, she volunteered to work as a nurse's aide at a one-thousand-bed American Red Cross Military Hospital in Beauvais, winning praise for her calmness tending to patients while under German bombardment. In late September, the sisters took a train to Belfort and reported to the nearby military hospital in Héricourt, a converted French army barracks that then housed six hundred flu-stricken American soldiers. There were very few doctors and not enough nurses. Assigned night duty, Cheney was given charge of three large wards and three smaller ones, becoming the de facto nurse, dispensing medications and giving injections, assisted by only two teenaged orderlies. Through eighteen long, exhausting nights, suffering and death were constants:

> *The second night Rosy sat straight up in bed and said the Lord's Prayer from beginning to end, then whimpered and trailed off into feeble curses and asked for a glass of beer, then died. A big fellow who looked like a Southern mountaineer in a bed facing the table where I worked, called "Mother, Mother" and when I went he took my hand and looked up at me happily and said "I saw yer smilin', Ma," and died. The little Irish barber who had fought courageously, got almost well and had a relapse and died. A fine looking boy by the window, who was not delirious and who seemed only humbly concerned not to be a bother, died smiling as though saying, "You must not feel badly." A man with a bad face began dreadfully to curse, saying the same thing over and over and over again. He struggled to get out of bed. The doctor came in and I helped tie the man's hands and feet to the ends of the bed and fasten a sheet tight over his body and tie it under the bed. Then the doctor began to put a gag in his mouth…He had a theory that a man who could not move became more tranquil and asked me the next night if it did not work. It had perfectly—at the end of the hour the monotonous curse had become fainter and fainter till it had trailed off to silence and the man was quiet forever.*[97]

Cheney returned to Manchester in March 1919 and missed the great pandemic's peak in Connecticut during the fall of 1918. Camp Devens, the major training area for Hartford draftees, was particularly hard hit. Nearly twelve thousand cases were reported by late September, and nurses and Red Cross volunteers from the Hartford area were summoned to help care for patients.

Hartford draftees began arriving in Europe with the new national army divisions. The 76th, or Liberty Bell, Division had been formed from conscripts from Upstate New York and New England, its 304th Infantry

Regiment composed largely of conscripts from the Hartford, Bridgeport and Waterbury immigrant communities, former factory workers who were taught English while in camp.[98] It reached France in July and functioned largely as a replacement division. One month before, the 77th, or Statue of Liberty, Division, which included Hartford-area draftees in its ethnically and geographically diverse ranks, became the first of the new divisions to take up frontline duty. The wave of new recruits also included formations of black troops. The vast majority of African Americans who saw service during World War I—367,710, including about 1,000 from Connecticut—were draftees. Most were assigned to construction or menial labor, either stateside or in Europe, in segregated units commanded by white general officers assisted by black subordinates. Two black divisions, the 92nd and the 93rd, assigned to the French army saw extensive combat during the war's late stages. Several black doughboys from Hartford served in the 92nd with the first battalion of the 367th Infantry, the "Buffaloes," which received a Croix de Guerre unit citation for gallantry. One member of the battalion, Private First Class Charles Henry Brown of Company B, a farm laborer in Berlin before the war, expressed justifiable pride in his wartime experience: "Proud to be a soldier & serve my Race & my Country," he wrote, recalling that in combat "when I went after a man I knew if I didn't get him—he'd get me, so I fought accordingly." The miseries of the western front recognized no color. Private James Andrew Sailor of Company E of the 367th had worked as a chauffer and repairman for Connecticut Tobacco Corporation in East Granby before he was drafted. He developed severe rheumatism and impaired eyesight from frontline service. "It made me no [sic] that I should have equal rights after going through the hard shift over there." Another infantryman, Private Robert L. Cole, Company G, 367th Infantry, who worked at Hartford Rubber Works before the war, returned home under treatment for shell shock, his state of mind having changed, he said, from "peaceful before but decidedly restless since." Many of Hartford's black veterans, like their white counterparts, drew positives from their experience, taking pride in doing their duty for their country and growing mentally and physically in the process. Sergeant Major Weaver Arvey Wood, of the 351st Field Artillery, 92nd Division, said the war left him "impressed by the brotherhood of man and disregard for social distinctions during mutual peril." Certainly, the paradox of living in Jim Crow America while waging war against tyranny abroad did not pass unnoticed. Hartford resident Corporal William Service Bell of the 546th Engineers found overseas service an improvement over camp life stateside, where "I was very aware of American democracy and [the] Negro's condition."[99]

On September 12, the AEF launched its first independent offensive, an attack by the American First Army on the German salient at St. Mihiel, south of Verdun. The three-day battle was a notable American victory, a prelude to the far greater, more ambitious Meuse-Argonne offensive. The men of the Yankee Division played a significant part in the success, which dislodged the Germans from their defensive positions and freed local French villages. Corporal Charles F. Coughlin, of Company F, 102nd Infantry, soon to be promoted to sergeant, described in a September 19 letter to his mother in Hartford how his company took a small hamlet near Mont Sec, bagging three hundred prisoners. The captives included the members of a military band "who had all their instruments with them, base drums and all…We go the whole bunch without losing a man."[100] Hartford resident Captain Stillman F. Westbrook, commander of a machine gun company assigned to the 104th Regiment, found the success nearly intoxicating. Westbrook wrote to his wife on September 15:

> *The victory was so complete, so far beyond expectations, that the morning of the 14th found us without prepared plans, so that in the adjustment of the forces, we were withdrawn and marched to the rear—not relieved exactly but held in reserve for some mysterious hush-hush move. And that is where we find ourselves now, a happy excited, thrilled lot of men. We are living in old German dugouts in the heart of the heights of the Meuse. It is lovely country, not unlike our own Connecticut Valley country, and it is remarkably peaceful in spite of our proximity to the line.[101]*

Westbrook's respite proved short-lived. His and his men were among 1.2 million AEF soldiers who took part in the massive offensive in the Meuse-Argonne, the greatest, most costly battle ever fought by the U.S. Army. Fought in the war's closing weeks, it left 26,277 Americans dead and 95,786 wounded. Remarkably, more Americans lost their lives in combat in September and October 1918 than during any month in either the Civil War or World War II.[102] On the opening day of the offensive, September 26, Sergeant Robert M. Ryans, twenty-six, of Company A, 102nd Infantry, was killed in action in what was described officially as a diversionary raid on the town of Marchéville. A native of Massachusetts, Ryans worked at Hartford Rubber Works and had joined Company A of the Connecticut National Guard First Infantry prior to the Mexican Punitive Expedition. At enlistment, according to his family, his birth name of Rines was changed and never corrected. He was decorated with the Croix de Guerre and the

Distinguished Service Cross and is buried in Arlington National Cemetery. Hartford resident Private Gustaf L. Johnson of Company F, 308th Infantry, 77th Division, was killed in action in the Argonne Forest on October 3, a day on which men from other companies in his regiment were fighting and dying and achieving lasting immortality as the Lost Battalion. Among thousands of casualties sustained by the 77th in the Meuse-Argonne were two New Britain residents: Private First Class Arthur J. Anderson, Company D, 306th Infantry, and Private Elmero Q. Anderson, of the 304th Field Artillery, both killed in October. A medic with the 306th Field Artillery, Private George W. Hanford of the Kensington section of Berlin, recalled one of the countless scenes of death and destruction experienced by the 77th Division in a letter to his mother on October 23:

> *Yesterday morning a hidden mine exploded and killed three men and wounded six men besides five or six horses. It was certainly one of the worst sights that I have seen and I have seen a good many since having been in the medical service at the Front. Such is one of the horrors of war back of the Front. In the years to come after the war I am afraid their* [sic] *will be many such accidents when farmers plow up their land etc.*[103]

Bronchial pneumonia probably resulting from the flu, not a German machine gun, claimed the life of Second Lieutenant Richard W. Ibell of the 301st Engineers, 76th Division. The New Britain native, a regular army veteran who spent eleven months in Mexico during the Punitive Expedition, died on October 24 at the Toul base hospital five days after being stricken in the line of duty. The 26th Division was kept in reserve during the initial phases of the great offensive but entered the fight in mid-October on the eastern side of the Meuse River, north of Verdun. Captain Westbrook described the terrain before going into action on October 16: "Desolation is everywhere. We had never seen such complete destruction of villages—Cumiers, Chattoncourt, Regneville, Neuville, Vacherauville and Samogneux—literally nothing left but the names; great gaping holes, made by shells of enormous caliber, were all that remained or all that showed of what must have been the usual picturesque communities."[104] Sergeant Coughlin wrote home on October 12 following his promotion. He had been visited by his uncle YMCA captain Matthew E. Coughlin, who arrived from division headquarters with $42,000 collected by Connecticut Spanish-American veterans to distribute to the state's servicemen, and was buoyed by rumors of peace. "I suppose there is great excitement at

Sergeant Charles F. Coughlin of Hartford, Company F, 102nd Infantry, 26th Division, died of wounds in the Meuse-Argonne. *Connecticut State Library.*

home now. I bet the old bells & whistles did some ringing & blowing when the news came through that Germany wanted peace."[105] It was his final letter. An Aetna employee who had become a popular player in Hartford amateur theatricals, Coughlin was wounded on October 23 and died four days later. Another Hartford native son, Private Louis F. Hart, twenty-three, a runner for the 101st Machine Gun Battalion, was mortally wounded on October 26. A replacement drafted in May 1918, he was "much pleased" to be assigned to the 101st "as he knew so many boys from Hartford,"[106] his mother, Elizabeth A. Hart, recalled. Hart was posthumously awarded the Distinguished Service Cross. On November 1, the massive American force finally began to break through the formidable German defensive lines, and the battle entered its final stages. Leading Company K of the 315th Regiment, 79th Division, was Harford native and veteran Connecticut guardsman John Thomas "Spike" Owens. Owens had enlisted in 1916 at age eighteen, was assigned to the 1st Infantry's machine gun company and remained with the company after the formation of the 102nd, in action continuously from February 1918 until late July, when he left the front lines for two months of officer training. The newly minted officer, just twenty years old, died on November 5 leading an attack on a German machine gun position. He was posthumously awarded the Distinguished Service Cross. On the war's last full day, November 10, Corporal George J. Gaudette of Company E, 102nd Infantry, died attempting to get aid for his pinned-down platoon. The New Britain man, who had enlisted in the company in May 1917 at age eighteen, was posthumously awarded the Distinguished Service Cross. He is one of 14,246 Americans interred in the Meuse-Argonne American Cemetery and Memorial at Romagne, the largest U.S. military cemetery in Europe.

Incredible as it sounds today, the fighting and dying continued until the moment the armistice took effect at 11:00 a.m. on November 11. A diarist with the 101ˢᵗ Machine Gun Battalion recorded the surreal nature of that instance:

> *The artillery is pounding harder than ever. We are waiting for 11 o'clock and as the time draws near, we look at our watches. Suddenly there is a queer silence—we don't know what to think or do. It is true—but no one wants to shout or laugh. We just cannot realize the significance of it. Here we were, only a few moments ago, ready to jump into our cars and go out and shoot up the Boche, or get shot up. What will happen, and where are we going now? Nothing happens, and we just light up another cigarette. Pretty soon a* Poilu *somewhat the worse for* cognac, *comes running out of dugout and shouts* "Fini la guerre!"—another, *also the worse for* cognac, *comes along the road driving a* camion. *He takes both hands from the wheel, waves them wildly, and shouts at the top of his lungs,* "Fini la guerre!"…The French are taking it more hilariously than the Yanks—but they have been fighting four years longer.*[107]*

The War Ends and the Heroes Return, November 1918–May 1919

"The greatest war in history ended this morning at 6 o'clock, Washington time," reported the *New Britain Herald* on the morning of November 11, 1918. By the time the *Herald*'s special edition hit the streets, it was already old news in the Hardware City. An AP bulletin received at the newspaper's office shortly before 3:00 a.m. local time had announced the signing of the armistice, and through the predawn hours, church bells rang, factory whistles sounded, impromptu parades formed and wary officials ordered the closing of saloons. Unlike four days earlier, when a false UPI report had touched off the premature "False Armistice" celebration, the news proved accurate, and so began one of the most memorable days in Hartford County history. In Manchester, local dignitaries began parading at 5:00 a.m. under streetlights. The parade in Bristol halted at the Bristol Village Green illuminated by a huge bonfire. Festivities in Collinsville village in the town of Canton included a funeral for the Kaiser, complete with a hearse, and the exuberant revelries in Southington forced a two-day shutdown of local factories. In the Connecticut capital, a crowd of onlookers began forming outside the *Courant*'s State Street office at 3:00 a.m. to catch the latest bulletins, their voices soon hoarse from cheering and singing patriotic anthems. Within an hour, downtown streets were filling up. "The spreading of the glad tidings was the quickest ever done in Hartford. No time was lost in getting hold of everybody who would get out of bed."[108] Over the din of parades and marching, the ringing of trolleys, the tooting of auto horns and the spectacle of hanging the Kaiser in effigy, newsboys scrambled to hawk special editions. Factories and schools closed for the day, as did the saloons, and city officials made final preparations for an evening Peace Parade, with the route ending in Bushnell Park beneath the capitol. In a proclamation to the "People of Hartford," Mayor Richard J. Kinsella expressed the feelings of many:

> *God is in the heavens and all is right with the world! Autocracy has been crushed and Democracy has been exalted. Never again will a deluded human being, intoxicated by the belief that he is a superman, from the vantage ground of a throne, crush the heads of his people in mad pursuit of abnormal ambition. The Kaiser in ignoble flight to save his own head is a picture that warms the hearts of the American people today.*[109]

The pent-up jubilation inspired by the announcement of the armistice followed a period of several anxious weeks. Local casualty lists had continued mounting through the fall, and the Spanish influenza had struck the Connecticut homefront with a vengeance, beginning in mid-September with initial reports from New London County. October marked the epidemic's deadliest month, with more than 5,000 flu-related deaths statewide. Hartford recorded 200 fatalities during the week of October

Black workers during an impromptu "False Armistice" parade in Hartford, November 7, 1918. *Connecticut State Library.*

Right: Hartford mayor Richard J. Kinsella. *Connecticut State Library*.

Below: Hartford Italians celebrate the armistice, November 11, 1918. *Connecticut State Library*.

15 and 550 for the month—a total representing two and a half times the number of the city's wartime service deaths.[110] The onslaught of patients led Hartford Hospital, on October 17, to open the Hartford Golf Club as an emergency flu hospital, staffed by volunteers because of the shortage of nurses. The numbers of the sick and dying prompted local officials in some Hartford County communities to close churches, schools and entertainment venues and cancel or curtail public events. Realizing the potential impact of the epidemic on the war effort, the State Council of Defense joined the Health Department in urging war bureaus and local committees to do everything possible to keep trained nurses in their home communities and began distribution of twenty thousand copies of the poster "Help Fight the Grippe, Kaiser Wilhelm's Ally" to publicize ways to protect against disease and limit its spread.[111] Area factories undertook their own precautions. At Arrow Electric in Hartford, where 30 percent of the workforce was stricken, the plant was ventilated twice a day, and volunteers drove employees with nursing training to the homes of their stricken brethren to aid in their care. In New Britain, which reported 342 flu deaths in October, work areas at Stanley Works were fumigated twice daily, and young women were hired to produce gauze facemasks for employees. Stanley workers were strongly advised to guard against spreading the disease by careless spitting, coughing or sneezing: "Do not spit on the floors, or around the factory or in public places, the company is providing proper receptacles. Spit in them."[112] By mid-November, coinciding with the ending of the war, the epidemic had begun to subside, and the number of new cases and recorded deaths fell sharply in Hartford County and statewide.

That the guns had stilled before the German military machine was thoroughly defeated was questioned by state leaders. Governor Holcomb, reelected to a third term in November, had argued for "unconditional surrender" by Germany; anything less, he wrote to a friend, amounted to "an asinine surrender to Germany duplicity. It would be a capital offense."[113] Holcomb publicly urged that United States stand firm with the Allies in demanding that terms of the peace "make Germany incapable of future mischief." A State Council of Defense poster, "Stand Fast America, Beware the Soft Pedal," played up the never-again theme.[114] As Connecticut State Guard commander Major General Lucien Burpee told a Plainville audience, "I would have liked to see the war carried into Germany. I would like to see their cities subjected, the people humbled, and the militarism crushed. Let them have felt what the Belgians and the French have felt. I had hoped to see the day when the American flag would float over Berlin, Germany."[115]

HELP FIGHT THE GRIPPE
KAISER WILHELM'S ALLY

How Not to GET It	How Not to GIVE It
GET FRESH AIR AND SUNSHINE. AVOID CROWDED PLACES, ESPECIALLY CARS. KEEP AWAY FROM SNEEZERS AND COUGHERS. DON'T VISIT PEOPLE ILL WITH COLDS. KEEP YOUR MOUTH AND TEETH CLEAN. PROTECT THE BODY BY PROPER CLOTHING. AVOID EXPOSURE TO SUDDEN CHANGES. AVOID WORRY, FEAR AND FATIGUE.	STAY AT HOME ON THE FIRST INDICATION OF A COLD. DON'T RECEIVE VISITORS WHILE SICK OR RECOVERING. DON'T LEAVE YOUR HOME UNTIL ALL SYMPTOMS HAVE GONE. DON'T SNEEZE, SPIT OR COUGH IN PUBLIC PLACES. DON'T HESITATE TO COMPLAIN AGAINST CARELESS COUGHERS AND SPITTERS.

THE STATE DEPARTMENT OF HEALTH AND THE CONNECTICUT STATE COUNCIL OF DEFENSE URGE YOU TO
DO YOUR BIT TO STOP THE GRIPPE

Public health officials in Hartford respond to the Spanish flu threat, 1918. *Simsbury Historical Society, Simsbury, Connecticut.*

The weeks following the armistice brought major adjustments, as Connecticut began dismantling its wartime bureaucracy and saw factory production orders cut back or cancelled, resulting in layoffs and work stoppages and raising tensions within the labor force. Alarmed government and business leaders worried about radical infiltration, particularly among the foreign born, and argued for continuation of Americanization initiatives. "We owe it to ourselves and to those who will succeed to our responsibilities and privileges to realize that Americanization is fundamentally a matter of self-defense and self-preservation and not one merely of sentiment or charitable impulse," Holcomb announced in his third inaugural address on January 8, 1919. He asked for the creation of a permanent state department of Americanization and was disappointed when the General Assembly chose instead to give the state board of education the authority.[116] By then, Americanization was deeply rooted at the local level, with seventy-seven committees up and running. Among the most active was the mayor's Americanization committee in Hartford. Volunteers from eighteen different city organizations—the YMCA, YWCA, the DAR, the Council of Jewish Women, Village Street Mission and the library among them—provided English instruction at night schools, in factories and in private homes.[117] But teaching English was only part of the committee's mission, explained committee secretary

Governor Holcomb inspects a captured German howitzer, date unknown. *Connecticut State Library.*

Howard Bradstreet: "Americanization is defined in the three letters that symbolize our country—U.S.A.—meaning to understand, to sympathize with and to assist."[118]

A bill introduced in the Connecticut General Assembly on April 1, 1919, repealed the wartime emergency powers granted Holcomb. With it ended the formal existence of the State Council of Defense, which had ceased all activities one month earlier, closed its offices in the capitol, tabulated expenses—it had spent $308,074.25 on war-related activities—and notified the war bureaus that its work was completed. The leave-taking and transition to peacetime had been gradual. Some former Council of Defense functions, like Americanization and the continued maintenance and preservation of wartime records, found new, permanent homes within the state bureaucracy. One of the first influential figures in the council to leave office had been Department of Publicity chairman George B. Chandler, who submitted a three-page resignation letter to Holcomb two weeks after the armistice. In it, Chandler warned about the uses and abuses of state-sponsored propaganda in a democratic society.

I believe that the operation of a Publicity Bureau by the Government is a dangerous practice in a Republic and one which can only be justified as a war measure. This belief has been strengthened and confirmed by my experiences…and my observations of the workings of similar agencies elsewhere. It is inevitable that sooner or later such bureaus will be used either to perpetuate the power of the persons directing them or to bolster the political enterprises or measures of certain individuals or groups…I do not care…to be responsible for a state-managed and state-financed publicity department beyond the period of war necessity.[119]

Chandler's powers of persuasion proved unneeded during the fifth and final liberty bond sale, the victory loan, in April 1919. Connecticut subscriptions exceeded the state's $66 million quota by 49.95 percent, the highest percentage of over-subscription in the country. In recognition of that accomplishment, on November 11, 1919, the first anniversary of the armistice, U.S. Treasury secretary Carter Glass awarded Connecticut the American flag that had flown over the nation's Capitol during the war. Hartford subscriptions in the victory loan totaled $35.8 million, bringing its total for all five loans to $133.8 million.[120]

Within weeks after hostilities ended, Hartford's soldiers, sailors and marines began returning home. Among the first were draftees with the greatly depleted 76th Division, the first national army division demobilized, whose members were discharged at Camp Devens beginning on December 18. Those held in German prison camps began arriving home in early 1919. Sergeant Joseph P. Nolan, twenty-four, a Hartford druggist who served with the medical detachment of the 102nd Infantry, had been taken prisoner at Seicheprey. After three weeks recuperating in an English hospital, he returned stateside on January 7, 1919, and was discharged at Camp Dix, New Jersey. Private William O'Sullivan, the Bristol man whose family mistakenly was informed of his death at Seicheprey, was released from camp four days after the armistice and discharged on January 18. Another Seicheprey captive from Company D of the 102nd, Sergeant Erving A. Dresser, returned to his unit after his release, serving until his discharge on April 29. Private Edward F. Clark of Canton was successfully treated for wounds after being taken prisoner at Seicheprey and was working on a prison farm at the time of the armistice. He was discharged from Camp Upton, New York, on April 1. One of Hartford's more celebrated POWs, Lieutenant John Jay Van Schaack of West Hartford, had been held since the bomber he was piloting was shot down behind German lines in August 1918. He and other freed American officers were transported by train to France in December, enjoying a festive trip through Switzerland en route. Apparently no worse for wear, Van Schaack visited Paris and found time for additional sightseeing in England and Scotland before ordered stateside.[121] He was discharged on February 27. After returning home, he and other local wartime aviators formed the Hartford Aero Club, which pioneered commercial and passenger aviation into the capital region.

For the men of the Yankee Division, the return home took several months. Exhausted and beaten down from unrelenting combat, they were relieved from frontline duty on November 14 and marched to a rear training area at Montigny-le-Roi in the Haute Marne to recover. There, on Christmas Day, they were visited by President Wilson and his wife, who eight days earlier had made a triumphal entry into Paris for the upcoming peace conference. The Wilsons had boarded a train early on the morning of December 25 for Chaumont, AEF headquarters, where they were greeted by an honor guard of the 102nd Infantry. A formal review of battalions and companies selected from among six American divisions, including the Yankee Division, was held at Humes village. Following Christmas Dinner with Yankee Division officers, the commander in chief visited enlisted billets, where it is believed he shook

The Welcome Home arch spanning Asylum Street in Hartford, 1919. *Connecticut State Library.*

the paw of the 102nd's famed mascot, Sergeant Stubby. A bull terrier so named because of his cropped tail, Stubby became America's greatest animal hero of the war. A stray, he had wandered into the regiment's camp at New Haven in the summer of 1917 and was adopted by Private James Robert Conroy of New Britain. Conroy succeeded in stowing his pet aboard ship when the regiment left for France. The dog became a great favorite, serving alongside the doughboys in the trenches, comforting the wounded and sniffing out those buried by shellfire. Stubby survived poison gas attacks and spent six weeks in a military hospital recovering from shrapnel wounds. He wore his own distinctive jacket, fashioned by female admirers in Château-Thierry and covered with military insignias and decorations, including the Iron Cross taken off a German soldier whom Stubby had captured in the Marchéville raid. After returning to the United States, Stubby spent two seasons as a college football mascot—Conroy had enrolled in law school in Washington, D.C.—and never left the media spotlight. He received numerous honors and was personally decorated by General Pershing. He visited Presidents Harding and Coolidge at the White House, and Stubby and Conroy became regulars at American Legion conventions. After Stubby's death in 1926, his remains were exhibited by the Red Cross and later donated by Conroy to the Smithsonian, where they remain today.[122]

Conroy, by then a corporal, and Stubby left Brest, France, with their regiment on March 31, 1919, aboard the *Agamemnon* bound for Boston Harbor. The transport, a former German vessel seized in 1917, carried about 5,000 doughboys, including veterans of two premier Connecticut units: the 102nd Infantry and the 101st Machine Gun Battalion. Welcoming them at dockside on April 7 were Connecticut governor Holcomb and Yale president Arthur T. Hadley, along with Boston mayor Andrew J. Peters and former Yankee Division commander Major General Edwards, who had been fêted in Hartford by city and Connecticut leaders one month before. Back on American soil, the men boarded waiting trains for Camp Devens. On April 25, the members of the fully re-formed Yankee Division marched for the final time before massive crowds aligning the streets of the Hub. Following their discharges, the division's Connecticut veterans joined other soldiers, marines, sailors, the state guard, the ceremonial Governor's Foot Guard and Putnam Phalanx, veterans of past conflicts and organized civilian contingents in a Welcome Home parade on April 30 in Hartford. Lined by an estimated 200,000 Connecticut residents, the route concluded at the state capitol with the presentation of colors to Governor Holcomb. Among the newly discharged was Corporal Thomas Erwin Carey of Company I, 102nd

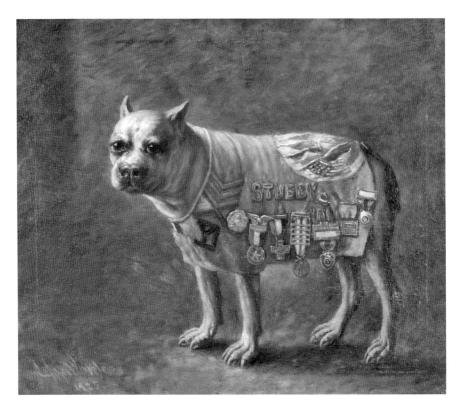

Above: Charles Ayer Whipple's painting of Stubby, hero dog mascot of the 102nd Infantry, 1925. *Joseph Brunjes/West Haven (Connecticut) Veterans Museum.*

Left: A "Welcome Home 26th (Yankee) Division" pin belonging to Major Morgan G. Bulkeley Jr. *Connecticut Historical Society, Hartford, Connecticut.*

Veterans of the 102nd Infantry marched along Trinity Street in Hartford's Welcome Home parade, April 30, 1919. *Connecticut State Library.*

Infantry. The New Britain native had seen continual action from March 3, 1918, to the armistice at Chemin-de-Dames, Seicheprey, Château Thierry, St. Mihiel and the Meuse-Argonne. Never wounded, he had survived gas attacks and a bout with Spanish flu and had just turned twenty years old on January 15, 1919. In answer to a question in a state military questionnaire about how his wartime experiences affected his state of mind, he wrote: "All the experience I have been through doesn't effect [*sic*] my mind at all. I just think of it as a dream, and forget all about it."[123]

THE GREAT WAR REMEMBERED

Memorials to those from the Hartford area who never made it back home began in 1919 and continued through the 1920s. On May 4, 1919, four days after the Welcome Home parade, a service hosted by the 1st Regiment of the Connecticut State Guard was held at the State Armory. The 2,500 in attendance listened to tributes to the fallen from several clergymen, including Protestant and Roman Catholic chaplains with the 102nd Infantry. Efforts by city officials to permanently recognize residents who died in service began in January 1920, when Mayor Richard J. Kinsella appointed a committee of three aldermen to work with park commissioners to find a suitable location for the planting of memorial trees in honor of each of the fallen. An appropriation of $2,000 was approved, and in the spring, 186 American elms, each with a wooden nametag assigned, were planted along both sides of the main drive through Colt Park. New mayor Newton C. Brainard formally dedicated the Trees of Honor Memorial on Flag Day, June 14, 1920, and schoolchildren laid wreaths beneath each sapling. The wooden tags were soon replaced by nine-inch-square wooden frames, each containing a bronze disc with the name of the deceased. However, within a few years, as additional names were added, markers deteriorated and trees relocated, representatives of the American Legion Rau-Locke Post 8 approached the Park Commission offering to underwrite the cost of new, permanent cast-iron plaques. The offer was accepted and 209 plaques cast. Measuring eight and a half by thirteen inches, the plaques were individually mounted on iron pipes with flag holders affixed, a project costing $2,000 to

$3,000. On each plaque was inscribed, "The American Legion Honors the Memory of," followed by the individual's name, rank, unit, date and place of wounds and date of death. Two of the named were civilians: William J. Hamersley, a Red Cross field director who died in October 1918 of complications from influenza contracted at Camp Devens, and Reverend John Brownlee Voorhees, a senior minister at Asylum Congregational Church who, while volunteering in France with the YMCA, was wounded by shellfire in June 1918 and died seven months later. Formal dedication of the revamped memorial was held on November 7, 1926. The Trees of Honor remained the city's premier World War I memorial, after plans for a massive $600,000 permanent structure in Bushnell Park collapsed amid municipal infighting on the eve of the Great Depression. Storm damage and Dutch elm disease eventually claimed the Colt Park elms. Sometime in the late 1960s, the plaques were removed and dumped unceremoniously in a park storage facility. There they lay, rusting and largely forgotten, until they were rediscovered in 2013. A project is currently underway to restore the plaques and find a new, permanent home for display.[124]

Other World War I memorials in Hartford County have fared better and remain prominent features of their communities. The World War I Memorial in New Britain, a 90-foot stone shaft topped by a sculpted double eagle, has stood majestically at Walnut Hill Park since its dedication on September 22, 1928. The design, by architect Harold Van Buren Magonigle of New York, was selected by a local committee following completion of his similar, much larger Liberty Memorial in Kansas City in 1926. Ground was broken for the memorial in April 1927, and the construction by Hayes Construction Co. of New Britain took about a year. A three-mile-long parade, witnessed by as many as 100,000 people, marked the dedication, which was attended by Governor John Trumbull, who had lost a brother on the *Lusitania*. On the semicircular parapet surrounding the monument shaft are mounted individual bronze plaques dedicated to each of the city's 123 service deaths, the names reflecting the broad ethnic diversity of a city that sent 4,000 residents into uniform during the war. On April 19, 1924, four years before the New Britain dedication, the City of Bristol had dedicated its own memorial, designed by local resident Harold A. Hayden: a 25-foot white granite shaft arising from a star-shaped base. On four of the five faces are the names of 48 residents who died in the conflict; below them are bronze plaques identifying nearly 1,300 city war veterans. The memorial was erected in the median of the divided, 4,400-foot-long Memorial Boulevard, dedicated three years earlier on November 11, 1921, on property donated by New Departure

A young girl studies one of the American Legion memorial plaques erected in Hartford's Colt Park in 1926. *Connecticut State Library.*

Manufacturing Co. founder, inventor-philanthropist Albert F. Rockwell. Major General Clarence R. Edwards attended the memorial dedication, held on the eve of the sixth anniversary of Seicheprey, the name adopted by the Bristol American Legion Post. The World War I monument remains today the centerpiece of the greatly expanded, twenty-five-acre Veterans Memorial Park and Boulevard.

In East Hartford, a bronze doughboy seven feet, four inches tall on a seventy-two-inch granite base has stood outside the Raymond Library on Main Street since its dedication on October 5, 1929. Cast by the American Bronze Company, the memorial, known as *Ready*, cost $7,000, which was raised through local donations, including $2,000 from schoolchildren.[125] Less

World War I Memorial in Walnut Hill Park, New Britain, Connecticut. *Author photograph.*

conspicuous stone memorials specific to local men and women who participated in the Great War or lost their lives doing so can be found in Windsor, Wethersfield and Glastonbury and in the Soldiers Field section of Northwood Cemetery in Hartford. A furious fundraising campaign, abetted by the Cheney family contributing 50 percent of the cost, enabled construction of Manchester Memorial Hospital, dedicated in 1920. A memorial to the forty-five Manchester men who died during the conflict was placed outside the hospital in 1933. A bronze statue of Major General Edwards has stood outside the state capitol since May 1942.

In addition to highly visible, permanent memorials, honor rolls containing the names of local men and women who served were compiled by war bureaus throughout Hartford County for display in town halls and municipal centers. Several communities, including Avon, Berlin, East Granby, Broad Brook and Warehouse Point in East Windsor, East Hartford, Glastonbury, New Britain and West Hartford, designed and struck their own service medals.[126] Memorials of a different sort began appearing with the formation of the American Legion. Organized by returning veterans of the American Expeditionary Forces and chartered by Congress, the legion

Above: Early postcard view of the World War I Memorial in New Britain. The pool was later drained. *New Britain Public Library.*

Left: World War I Monument at the Veterans Memorial Park and Boulevard, Bristol, Connecticut. *Author photograph.*

held its Connecticut organizational meeting at the City Club in Hartford on June 10, 1919. There, an executive committee approved filing articles of incorporation, adopted a charter and bylaws and elected temporary officers to serve until the state convention in October. "After today, you are going to see The American Legion grow in this state like a mushroom," declared Executive Committee chairman James B. Moody Jr. of Hartford. "We have already received petitions for charters from local organizations representing a total membership of nearly 3,000 men. We should have more than 10,000 members in Connecticut posts before the first state convention."[127] The legion's second chartered post in Connecticut and first in Hartford County was the Seicheprey Post; the sixth state post, Eddy-Glover, was established in New Britain. Hartford claimed Post No. 7, Jane A. Delano, named in memory of the founder of the American Red Cross Nursing Service and chartered by Hartford servicewomen, and No. 8, Rau-Locke, which memorialized the city's two slain officer-heroes of the war and quickly became one of the state's largest, most influential posts. By the end of 1919, fifteen of seventy-five of the legion's chartered posts in Connecticut were in Hartford County, most taking the names of local men who had died. The legion took a leading role in providing assistance to returning Connecticut veterans and was charged with administering the $2.4 million Soldier's, Sailors and Marines Fund established by the Connecticut General Assembly in 1919 to aid needy veterans and their families. In Hartford, the legion took over management of the popular Soldiers, Sailors and Marine Club established by the city in newly renovated quarters previously used by the draft board in the Halls of Record building.

Through the 1920s and 1930s, the Great War continued to cast a shadow on those in the Hartford region touched most directly by it. The Hartford Exiles, a group whose members had served with AEF auxiliaries, such as the YMCA, Knights of Columbus, the Red Cross and the press corps, reveled in their shared experience at an annual New Year's Day banquet in the city. The date recognized the Exiles' founding on January 1, 1919, at the American Grill room of the Hotel Regina in Paris; the annual banquet typically featured music and guest speakers and received respectful coverage from the city's newspapers. Gatherings of a more somber nature began in May 1930, with pilgrimages by thousands of the nation's Gold Star mothers and widows to Europe to visit the graves of loved ones. The visitations, via liners leaving New York Harbor, were paid for by the U.S. government and carefully scripted by the War Department. A total of 166 Connecticut mothers and widows, including 40 from Hartford County, were determined

Ready statue in front of the Raymond Library, Main Street, East Hartford, Connecticut. *Author photograph.*

Above: Dedication of the American Legion memorial to the Hartford World War I dead buried overseas, 1938, Soldiers Field, Northwood Cemetery, Hartford. *Connecticut State Library.*

Left: Plaque on the American Legion memorial to the Hartford World War I dead, Soldiers Field, Northwood Cemetery, Hartford. *Author photograph.*

eligible for the trips, which peaked in 1930 and 1931 and continued until October 1933. About two dozen local women from Hartford, New Britain, Bristol, Manchester, Enfield, Farmington, Wethersfield, West Hartford and Windsor participated, including Frances Rau, the widow of Major Rau, one of 81 servicemen from Hartford left buried overseas or lost at sea.[128]

For many local veterans, the wartime experience left deep scars, which the annual patriotic parades, Memorial and Armistice Day tributes and the bonhomie of those who served with them could not conceal. Some, like Raymond J. Meegan, the city's deputy sealer of weights and measures, were left permanently disabled by combat. He was elected commander of the Connecticut Disabled Veterans of the World War and was only thirty years old when he died tragically in a traffic accident on New Year's Eve 1927.[129] Others, like Morgan G. Bulkeley Jr., scion of the Bulkeley family, never recovered from the debilitating effects of poison gas and disease. Bulkeley, who commanded the 101st Machine Gun Battalion, was working as vice-president and treasurer of Aetna Life Insurance at the time of his premature death in 1926 at age forty.[130] Many others carried searing emotional or psychological baggage or struggled to adjust to the demands of peacetime. Connecticut boasted the nation's first state home for veterans, Fitch's Home for Soldiers and Their Orphans, which had opened in Darien, Connecticut, during the Civil War and was taken over by the state in 1888, a few years after the death of its founder, Benjamin Fitch. By 1930, state veterans officials realized that Fitch's Home was woefully inadequate to meet the needs of the World War I generation, particularly as those needs were mounting as the nation plunged into the Depression. In December 1931, the Commission for the Establishment of a Soldiers Home, chaired by Benedict M. Holden, former member of the wartime Military Emergency Board, met in Hartford and voted to build a new facility in southern Hartford County on 310 acres of farmland in Rocky Hill. The property, owned by Hartford Retreat, contained several buildings used for staff housing, and its proximity to the Veterans Administration Hospital in Newington was a selling point. By late August 1932, with Fitch's unable to contain the Depression-fueled overflow, some 140 homeless veterans, including several Bonus Marchers, were living on the Rocky Hill grounds in buildings and tents: "On the model farm there, a man who served Connecticut in the war is given a chance to rebuild himself physically, mentally and morally," reported the *Courant*.[131] Construction of a permanent facility on the property, designed to accommodate 1,000 veterans, began in the late 1930s, with a U.S. Public Works Administration (PWA) grant supplying 45 percent of the funding. The

$3.5 million project—with barracks-style dormitories for veterans, housing for nurses and staff, an administration building, an auditorium, a chapel and an infirmary—was completed in August 1940. A special train brought the Fitch's residents to their new home. At its dedication on September 15, more than 500 residents of the new Veterans Home and Hospital—more than 90 percent of whom were World War I veterans—listened as Governor Raymond E. Baldwin paid them tribute. "We owe an obligation difficult to measure and impossible to pay fully," he said.[132]

Notes

Introduction

1. Dr. Chad Williams, One Century Later panel discussion, *U.S. World War I Centennial Commission Meetings and Public Programs, Sunday, July 27, 2014.*
2. Beals, *Making of Bristol,* 200.

Chapter 1

3. *Weekly Gazette of East Hartford,* "Off to Europe: Gazette Party Leaves for a Seven Weeks Tour," July 3, 1914.
4. Henry B. Hale, "War Faced Gazette Party: No Hardships Encountered but a Scramble for Home Made Necessary," *Weekly Gazette of East Hartford,* August 28, 1914; *Hartford Courant,* "*Nieuw Amsterdam* in Quarantine: Stopped Many Times by Atlantic Patrols—2,000 Passengers," August 18, 1914.
5. *Hartford Times,* August 10, 1914.
6. Fraser, "Patriot Society," 15.
7. Mann, *Kate: The Woman Who Was Hepburn,* 24.
8. Mayor's Annual Message to Common Council, April 17, 1916, Box 216, Folder 2, Mayor and Council Papers.
9. Decker, *Hartford Immigrants,* 103–4.

10. Daniel D. Bidwell, "The Present Outlook in the Ulster Situation," *Hartford Courant*, July 12, 1914.

11. *Hartford Courant*, "Many Hear Talks at After-Meeting," May 3, 1914.

12. Daniel D. Bidwell, "How London Takes the War," *Hartford Courant*, August 24, 1914.

13. *Hartford Courant*, "Bidwell Talks on Worldwide War," October 27, 1914; ibid., "Wienerwurst Story Told to Bankers," October 28, 1914; *New York Times*, "Saw Germans in Lille: New Yorker in the Town When the Invaders Took Possession," September 7, 1914.

14. *New York Times*, "Canadian Soldiers Were Insured Here: Metropolitan and Aetna Life Took Risks on 16,000 for $14,000,000," May 28, 1916.

15. Frazar B. Wilde speech, January 1960, Aetna archives, file 3-7703.

CHAPTER 2

16. *Hartford Courant*, "Mrs. Pankhurst Gets to Town: Notorious Militant Keeps Followers Waiting," November 13, 1913. Information about Pope's background from Katz, *Dearest of Geniuses*.

17. Ramsay, *Lusitania*, 56; *Hartford Courant*, "Connecticut Goods on the *Lusitania*," May 11, 1915.

18. Theodate Pope to Ada Pope, June 28, 1915, Theodate Pope Riddle Archive.

19. Elizabeth Collins, Hill-Stead Museum researcher, e-mail message to author, May 10, 2015.

20. *Hartford Courant*, "Trumbull Co. to Make Arms to Avenge Death," May 11, 1915.

21. Ibid., "Travelers' Record Loss on *Lusitania*," May 20, 1915.

22. Meeting Minutes for May 12, 1915, RG 125, Box 1, Connecticut Peace Society Records.

23. *Hartford Courant*, "German-Americans Appeal to Public: Hartford Societies Adopt Resolutions on the War," August 14, 1914.

24. Ibid., "Great Crowd Packs Parsons Theater: Hear '*Die Wach am Rhein*' and 'Star-Spangled Banner,'" February 2, 1915.

25. *New Britain Herald*, "Women to Organize: Will Help German Children Left Destitute By the War," August 19, 1916.

26. *Hartford Courant*, "Hartford Germans Send a Petition to Congress," April 24, 1916.

27. *New York Times*, "First of American Legion Off for Flanders," May 28, 1916.

28. *Hartford Courant*, "Thompsonville Has Many Burglaries: Italians Go for Enlistment," August 1, 1915.

29. Daniel D. Bidwell, "Vast Expansion in Hartford During War May Be Matched by Prosperity of Peace," *Hartford Courant*, June 29, 1919.

30. Orders from Foreign Governments, Series IV, Box 23, RG 103, Colt Patent Fire Arms Manufacturing Co. Records; Segel, "U.S. Colt Vickers Model of 1915," 1–2.

31. *Hartford Courant*, "Thomson, Fenn & Co. Furnish Valuable Table: Shows Comparative List Prices as of June 29, 1915 and June 27, 1916 of Local Manufacturing, Insurance, Public Utilities and Bank Stocks," July 2, 1916.

32. Ibid.

33. Slotkin, *Lost Battalions*, 31.

34. *Hartford Courant*, "Preparedness for Trinity Alumni: Object of Movement Started by Graduate Committee," April 14, 1916.

35. Ibid., "17,000 March for Preparedness in Monster Parade While 100,000 Spectators Throng City's Streets and Cheer Wonderful 'America First' Demonstration," June 4, 1916.

36. "Aetna Life at the 'Front' as Usual," undated, Aetna archives, file 3-7703.

CHAPTER 3

37. *Hartford Courant*, "Governor Hears of Plots Against U.S. in Hartford," March 22, 1917. The speech was reported in several newspapers, including the *Hartford Times*.

38. Ibid., "German Agents Work in Hartford on Minds of Alien Drill Groups," March 23, 1917.

39. Ibid., "Honesty, Industry and Sobriety, the Moto of Governor-Elect Holcomb," January 3, 1915. Biographical information about Holcomb can be found on "Marcus Hensey Holcomb: Governor of Connecticut, 1915–1921," Connecticut State Library, www.cslib.org/gov/holcomb.htm.

40. Marcus Holcomb to Carl Laemmle, December 11, 1917, file 108; Holcomb to Mr. Phillips, August 26, 1918, file 124; Holcomb to J.B. Thwing, June 25, 1918, file 49, Marcus H. Holcomb Papers, Numerical Files 1917–18.

41. *Hartford Courant*, "Governor Holcomb's Preparedness Message," February 7, 1917.

42. Report of the Military Census Board, March 31, 1917; reports from Bristol Census commissioner Henry E. Cottle, Bloomfield commissioner George F. Humphrey and Granby commissioner Eugene E. Goddard, Boxes 1 and 5, RG 029, Military Census Bureau Records.
43. Unsigned memorandum by state librarian George S. Godard, August 30, 1918, Box 2, Military Census Bureau Records.
44. *Hartford Courant*, "Seven Incendiary Fires Cause $36,000 Loss in New Britain," February 22, 1917; Thibodeau, *New Britain*, 65–66.
45. *Hartford Courant*, "72-Years-Old Man Enlists in Guard," April 14, 1917, http://www.search.proquest.com.
46. Fraser, "Yankees at War," 147–48.
47. *Hartford Courant*, "Work of Fire Insurance Companies of Great Value to the Government," April 1, 1917.
48. Ibid., "University Club Hears Governor," April 4, 1917.
49. Ibid., "Home Guard Purpose Explained," March 26, 1917.
50. Burpee, *History of Hartford County Connecticut*, 2:791.

CHAPTER 4

51. *Bristol Press*, "Events Move Rapidly," April 7, 1917.
52. *Hartford Times*, "The Cost to You," April 6, 1917.
53. Ibid., "Hartford Pledges Allegiance; Will Place Men and Material at Command of U.S. Government," April 7, 1917.
54. Slotkin, *Lost Battalions*, 74.
55. Mayor's Annual Message to Common Council, May 13, 1918, Box 216, Folder 4, Mayor and Council Papers.
56. *Hartford Courant*, "America Registers for War with Spirit and Without Disorder," June 6, 1917.
57. Ibid., "Crowder Is Asked for Equal Draft Apportionments," August 5, 1917.
58. *New Britain Herald*, "Thundering Farewell to City's Big Draft Quota," September 20, 1917.
59. *Hartford Courant*, "Militia Should Be Taken from Guard Duty; Put in Training Camps," June 20, 1917.
60. Ibid., "Rallies Bring Forth Nearly 200 Applicants for Army Enlistment," June 29, 1917.
61. Ibid., "Women Start Work for Liberty Loan," May 27. 1917.
62. Ibid., "Liberty Loan Goes Far Beyond Goal Line in Windup Campaign," June 16, 1917.

63. Bissell, *Report of the Connecticut State Council of Defense*, 32.

64. *Hartford Times*, "Chorus Singing for War Ardor," October 18, 1917.

65. *Hartford Courant*, "15,000 Cheer Roosevelt as He Declares America Will 'Fight to Finish,'" November 3, 1917.

66. *Hartford Times*, "Thousands at War-Time Rally," November 3, 1917.

67. *Hartford Courant*, "Tobacco Men Are Pledged to Grow More Crops," April 22, 1917.

68. Ibid., "Connecticut's Food Organization Ready for Big Spring Drive," March 31, 1918.

69. Quoted in Thibodeau, *New Britain*, 67.

70. *Weekly Gazette of East Hartford*, "Hens That Help the Enemy," August 16, 1918.

71. *Hartford Courant*, "D.A.R. Chapter Urges Martial Law," December 14, 1917.

72. Ibid., "Dr. Luther Wants Industrial Draft," April 11, 1918.

73. Lucien F. Burpee to Marcus Holcomb, June 18, 1918, Marcus H. Holcomb Papers, file 117.

74. Assistant Secretary A.B. Sands of State Council of Defense, "To the Librarians," July 12, 1918, Ephemera box 2 Watkinson Library World War I Collection.

75. *Hartford Courant*, "Home Guard Lines Up Socialists for Loyalty; To Watch All Meetings," April 8, 1918.

76. Ibid., "Personnel of New Committee to Aid Foreigners Here," October 2, 1917.

77. Ibid., "Americanization Center Established," July 21, 1918.

78. Manufacturers' Assn. of Connecticut, *Our Job: To the Factory Workers of Connecticut*, 1–5.

79. General manager B.H. Blood, Pratt & Whitney Co., Industrial Survey questionnaires, reports 1918, boxes 64 and 65, RG 029, Military Census Bureau Records.

80. *Hartford Courant*, "Hartford's Industrial War Work Accomplishment for the Government," January 26, 1919.

81. *Stanley Workers* 1, no. 1 (November 1, 1917).

82. *Hartford Courant*, "Risked Lives in State Making Poisonous Gas to Smother German Army," February 18, 1919.

83. Ibid., "Record-Breaking Parade Marks City's Third Loan Triumph," May 5, 1918.

Chapter 5

84. Neeld to Phillips, November 14–19, 1960, Connecticut Historical Society.

85. Quoted in Spiess and Bidwell, *History of Manchester*, 258.

86. Lyman Michaels to Alta Crowley, April 24, 1918, Memorial Military Museum.

87. *Hartford Courant*, "Vivid Description of Bristol Boys' Part in the Fighting," May 20, 1918. The report mistakenly published Dresser's last names as "Dressing."

88. Sibley, *With the Yankee Division in France*, 144.

89. *Hartford Courant*, "Lieut. Robinson Died Blazing Away with 2 Automatics," May 18, 1919.

90. Ibid., "Tells of Death of Thompsonville Man," August 23, 1918.

91. Strickland, *Connecticut Fights*, 189.

92. *Hartford Courant*, "101st M.G.B. Cut Hun Line Under Heavy Fire," October 20, 1918.

93. Quoted in Shay, *Yankee Division*, 124

94. *Hartford Courant*, "Major George J. Rau Killed on Battlefield July 25," August 7, 1918.

95. Ruth Hovey to Alice Huntley Hovey, July 18, 1918, from Ruth Hovey, *Connecticut Military Questionnaires, 1919–1920*.

96. Frank Kenneth Young, *Connecticut Military Questionnaires, 1919–1920*.

97. Cheney, *Memories*, 72–73.

98. Gutierrez, "Connecticut Doughboy's Requiem," 58.

99. Charles Henry Brown, James Andrew Sailor, Robert L. Cole, Weaver Arvey Wood and William Service Bell, *Connecticut Military Questionnaires, 1919–1920*.

100. Charles F. Coughlin to Sarah Coughlin, September 19, 1918, Coughlin and Coughlin, Correspondence and Memorabilia.

101. Westbrook, "Those Eighteen Months," 174–75.

102. Keene, *World War I*, 19–20.

103. George W. Hanford to Mrs. Frank Hanford, October 23, 1918, Connecticut Soldiers Collection.

104. Westbrook, "Those Eighteen Months," 190–91. Names and spellings of villages have been left as recorded.

105. Charles Coughlin to Sarah Coughlin, October 23, 1918, Coughlin and Coughlin, Correspondence and Memorabilia.

106. Louis F. Hart, *Connecticut Military Questionnaires, 1919–1920*.

107. Wainwright, *History of the 101st Machine Gun Battalion*, 132–33.

CHAPTER 6

108. *Hartford Courant*, "Hartford Begins Wild Celebration in Honor of Ending the War," November 11, 1918.

109. *Hartford Evening Post*, "God in Heaven Says Kinsella: Mayor's Proclamation Urges All to Give Thanks for Victory," November 11, 1918.

110. Arcari and Birden, "1918 Influenza Epidemic in Connecticut," 37.

111. *Hartford Courant*, "Health Board Starts Anti-Grip Campaign," October 6, 1918.

112. *Stanley Workers* 1, no. 26 (October 17, 1918).

113. Marcus Holcomb to Norris G. Osborn, October 14, 1918, Marcus H. Holcomb Papers, file 89.

114. *Hartford Courant*, "Governor Warns Against Solf's Whining Notes," December 6, 1918.

115. Ibid., "Regrets Germany Signed Armistice in Memorial Talk," December 23, 1918.

116. Ibid., "Americanization Is Self-Preservation, Says Holcomb," January 9, 1919.

117. Ibid., "Americanization Conference Held," March 17, 1919.

118. Ibid., "Americanization Defined in Three Letters—U.S.A.," April 4, 1919.

119. George W. Chandler to Marcus Holcomb, November 25, 1918, Marcus H. Holcomb Papers, file 107.

120. *Hartford Courant*, "Hartford Subscribed $134,000,000 in Five Liberty Loan Drivers," May 28, 1919.

121. Ibid., "Shot Down in Bombing Plane, He Lands in Hun Prison Camp," March 23, 1919.

122. Bausum, *Sergeant Stubby*, 215–21.

123. Thomas Erwin Carey, *Connecticut Military Questionnaires, 1919–1920*

CHAPTER 7

124. Ferrari and Secord, "Restoring Hartford's Lost WWI Memorial," 42–43; Yerrington, *Memorial to the Men of Hartford*; Memorials, World War I, Proposed Plans, Box 387, Folder 19, Mayor and Council Papers.

125. Inventories of American Painting and Sculpture database, "*Ready* (sculpture)."

126. *Hartford Courant*, "Town Service Medals in State Library," March 20, 1921.

127. Minutes of First Department Executive Meeting, Hartford, June 10, 1919, American Legion Connecticut Department.

128. *Hartford Courant*, "Hartford's Gold Star Pilgrimage," June 8, 1930; ibid., "18 in State to Take Gold Star Voyages," March 22, 1931.

129. Ibid., "Raymond Meegan Killed as Auto Truck Hits Pole," January 1, 1928.

130. Ibid., "Maj. Bulkeley Dies After Long Illness at His Home," March 23, 1926.

131. Ibid., "A Haven of Refuge for Jobless Veterans," August 21, 1932.

132. Ibid., "Tribute Paid to Veterans by Governor," September 15, 1940.

SELECTED BIBLIOGRAPHY

The following lists principal sources used in preparation of this manuscript. Specific newspaper articles relied upon as sources of information or quoted material are cited in the notes.

ARCHIVAL SOURCES

Aetna World War I Collection. Aetna Inc., Hartford, Connecticut.

American Legion Department of Connecticut Archives, Rocky Hill, Connecticut.

Colt's Patent Fire Arms Manufacturing Company Records, 1810–1980. Connecticut State Library, Hartford.

Connecticut Peace Society Records, 1910–21. Connecticut State Library.

Connecticut Soldiers Collection, George W. Hanford Papers. Thomas J. Dodd Research Center, University of Connecticut, Storrs.

Connecticut State Council of Defense Records, 1917–19. State Archives. Connecticut State Library.

Coughlin, Matthew E., and Charles F. Coughlin. Correspondence and Memorabilia, 1879–1921. Connecticut Historical Society, Hartford.

Ensign-Bickford Collection. Simsbury Free Library, Simsbury, Connecticut.

Marcus H. Holcomb Papers, 1915–21. State Archives. Connecticut State Library.

Mayor and Council Papers. Hartford Town and City Clerk Archives. Hartford History Center, Hartford Public Library.

Memorial Military Museum, Bristol, Connecticut.

Military Census Bureau Records, 1917–20. State Archives. Connecticut State Library.

Neeld, Lawrence, Hartford, Connecticut, to Edward Hake Phillips, Sherman, Texas, November 14–19, 1960. Connecticut Historical Society, Hartford.

New Britain Industrial Museum Collection. New Britain, Connecticut.

Theodate Pope Riddle Archive. Hill-Stead Museum, Farmington, Connecticut.

Watkinson Library World War I Collection. Trinity College, Hartford, Connecticut.

Books

Barry, John M. *The Great Influenza: The Epic Story of the Deadliest Plague in History*. New York: Penguin Books, 2004.

Bausum, Ann. *Sergeant Stubby: How a Stray Dog and His Best Friend Helped Win World War I and Stole the Heart of a Nation*. Washington, D.C.: National Geographic, 2014.

Beals, Carleton. *The Making of Bristol*. Bristol, CT: Bristol Library Association, 1954.

Burpee, Charles W. *History of Hartford County Connecticut, 1633–1928: Being a Study of the Makers of the First Constitution and the Story of their Lives, of Their Descendants and of All Who Have Come*. 3 vols. Chicago: S.J. Clarke Publishing, 1928.

Cheney, Dorothy. *Memories, November, 1917–March, 1919*. Hartford, CT: Finlay Brothers, 1929.

Decker, Robert Owen. *Hartford Immigrants: A History of the Christian Activities Council (Congregational), 1850–1980*. New York: United Church Press, 1987.

Grant, Ellsworth S. *Yankee Dreamers and Doers: The Story of Connecticut Manufacturing*. 2nd ed. N.p.: Connecticut Historical Society & Fenwick Productions, 1996.

Grant, Ellsworth Strong, and Marion Hepburn Grant. *The City of Hartford 1784–1984: An Illustrated History*. Hartford: Connecticut Historical Society, 1986.

Hallas, James H. *Doughboy War: The American Expeditionary Force in World War I*. Boulder, CO: Lynne Rienner Publishers, 2000.

Harries, Meirion, and Susie Harries. *The Last Days of Innocence: America at War, 1917–1918*. New York: Random House, 1997.

Hills, Ratcliffe M. *The War History of the 102d Regiment, United States Infantry, Presented by the Regimental Machine Gunners*. Hartford, CT: Ratcliffe M. Hills, historian, 1924.

Janick, Herbert F., Jr. *A Diverse People: Connecticut 1914 to the Present*. Chester, CT: Pequot Press, 1975.

Katz, Sandra L. *Dearest of Geniuses: A Life of Theodate Pope Riddle*. Windsor, CT: Tide-mark Press, 2003.

Keegan, John. *The First World War*. New York: Alfred A. Knopf, 1998.

Keene, Jennifer D. *World War I: The American Soldier Experience*. Lincoln: University of Nebraska Press, 2011.

Lengel, Edward G. *To Conquer Hell: The Meuse-Argonne, 1918*. New York: Henry Holt, 2008.

Mann, William J. *Kate: The Woman Who Was Hepburn*. New York: Henry Holt & Co, 2006.

Mead, Gary. *The Doughboys: America and the First World War*. Woodstock, NY: Overlook Press, 2000.

Ramsay, David. Lusitania*: Saga and Myth*. New York: W.W. Norton, 2001.

Scott, Emmett J. *Scott's Official History of the American Negro in the World War*. Chicago: Homewood Press, 1919.

Shay, Michael E. *The Yankee Division in the First World War: In the Highest Tradition*. College Station: Texas A&M University Press, 2008.

Sibley, Frank P. *With the Yankee Division in France*. Boston: Little, Brown, 1919.

Slotkin, Richard. *Lost Battalions: The Great War and the Crisis of American Nationality*. New York: Henry Holt and Co., 2005.

Spiess, Mathias, and Percy W. Bidwell. *History of Manchester, Connecticut*. South Manchester, CT: W.H. Schieldge, 1924

Sterner, Daniel. *Vanished Downtown Hartford*. Charleston, SC: The History Press, 2013.

Strickland, Captain Daniel W. *Connecticut Fights: The Story of the 102nd Regiment*. New Haven, CT: Quinnipiack Press, 1930.

Thibodeau, Patrick. *New Britain: The City of Invention*. Chatsworth, CA: Windsor Publications Inc., 1989.

Van Dusen, Albert E. *Connecticut*. New York: Random House, 1961.

Wainwright, Philip S., ed. *History of the 101st Machine Gun Battalion*. Hartford, CT: 101st Machine Gun Battalion Association, 1922.

Westbrook, Stillman F. *Those Eighteen Months: October 9, 1917–April 8, 1919: From the War Letters of Stillman F. Westbrook, Published for Private Distribution to the Men of the Machine Gun Company of the 104th Infantry, 26th Division, American Expeditionary Forces*. Hartford, CT: Lockwood & Brainard, 1934.

Yerrington, Charles B. *Memorial to the Men of Hartford Who Died in Service During the World War, 1917–1918*. Hartford, CT: Charles B. Yerrington, 1927.

OTHER PUBLICATIONS

Arcari, Ralph D., and Hudson Birden. "The 1918 Influenza Epidemic in Connecticut." *Connecticut History* 38, no. 1 (Fall 1997–Spring 1999): 28–43.

Bissell, Richard M., chairman. *Report of the Connecticut State Council of Defense, December 1918.* Hartford: Connecticut State Council of Defense, 1919.

Coan, Francis M. "A Few Men in the Great War: The Experiences of the Soldiers of Company D (Bristol): 1st Connecticut National Guard Regiment, March 1917–April 1918." Master's thesis, Central Connecticut State University, 1990.

Connecticut Department of Labor and Factory Inspection. *Report on the Department of Labor on the Conditions of Wage-Earners in the State: Printed in Compliance with Statute.* Hartford, CT: published by the state, 1918.

Ferrari, Lynn, and Greg Secord. "Restoring Hartford's Lost WWI Memorial." *Connecticut Explored* 13, no. 3 (Summer 2015): 42–43.

Fraser, Bruce. "The Patriot Society: Cultural Absolutism in Connecticut, 1917–1918." Master's thesis, Columbia University, 1971.

———. "Yankees at War: Social Mobilization on the Connecticut Homefront, 1917–1918." PhD diss., Columbia University, 1976.

Gutierrez, Edward Anthony. "A Connecticut Doughboy's Requiem: The Experience of the World War I Connecticut Soldier." Master's thesis, Trinity College, 2004.

Magnell, A.E. "New Britain's Part in the World War." Program, *New Britain's Welcome Home to Her Service Men, Sept. 15–20, 1919.* New Britain, CT: Chamber of Commerce, 1919.

Office of the Adjutant General, State Armory, Hartford, CT. *Service Records: Men and Women in the Armed Forces of the United State During World War 1917–1920.* 3 vols. New Haven, CT: United Printing Services, 1941(?).

Stanley Workers, biweekly wartime newsletter of the Stanley Works, vol. 1, nos. 1–28. New Britain Industrial Museum, New Britain, Connecticut.

U.S. Bureau of the Census. *Fourteenth Census of the United States, 1920 Bulletin. Population of Connecticut by Number of Inhabitants by Counties and Minor Civil Divisions.* Washington, D.C.: Government Printing Office, 1920.

———. *Fourteenth Census of the United States Taken in the Year 1920, Vol. III. Population 1920.* Washington, D.C.: Government Printing Office, 1922.

———. *Thirteenth Census of the United State Taken in the Year 1910, Vol. II. Population 1910.* Washington, D.C.: Government Printing Office, 1913.

NEWSPAPERS

Bristol Press
Hartford Courant, http://www.search.proquest.com
Hartford Evening Post
Hartford Times
New Britain Herald
New York Times, http://www.search.proquest.com
Weekly Gazette of East Hartford

ELECTRONIC SOURCES

American Battle Monuments Commission (ABMC). ABMC website. http://www.abmc.gov/cemeteries-memorials#.VYgh72dFBjp.

Ancestry.com. *Connecticut Military Census, 1917*. Provo, UT: Ancestry.com Operations Inc., 2012. http://search.ancestry.com.

———. *Connecticut Military Questionnaires, 1919–1920*. Provo UT: Ancestry.com Operations Inc., 2013. http://search.ancestry.com.

Blanchard, Ralph. "The History of the YMCA in World War I." http://www.worldwar1.com/dbc/ymca.htm.

Bruce, Robert. "Machine Guns of WWI: SADJ Commemorates the 100th Anniversary of World War I." *Small Arms Defense Journal* 6, no. 3 (November 21, 2014). http://www.sadefensejournal.com/wp/?p=2782.

Doughboy Center: The Story of the American Expeditionary Forces. "Regimental, Select Battalions & Support Train Numbers for AEF Divisions." http:///www.worldwar1.com/dbc/unitnumbers.htm.

Fold3.com. "Service Record, Connecticut: Men and Women in the Armed Forces of the United State During World War, 1917–1920," 2013. http://www.fold3.com.

Inventories of American Painting and Sculpture database, Smithsonian American Art Museum, Control #IAS CT000067. "*Ready* (sculpture)," accessed through Smithsonian Institution Research Information System (SIRIS), http://siris-artinventories.si.edu.

Manufacturers' Association of Connecticut. Our Job: To the Factory Workers of Connecticut. Hartford: Manufacturers' Association of Connecticut, 1918. http://worldcat.org/ocic/18480618/viewonline.

One Century Later panel discussion. J.C. Nichols Auditorium, 1 hour, 12 min., 53 sec. From National World War I Museum at Liberty Memorial, Kansas City, Missouri. *U.S. World War I Centennial Commission Meetings and*

Public Programs, Sunday, July 27, 2014. http://theworldwar.org/explore/centennial-comm.

Pelland, Dave. "Memorial Boulevard, Bristol (Part 1)." CT Monuments.net, July 19, 2011. http://ctmonuments.net/2011/07/memorial-boulevard-bristol-part-1.

Remembering World War One: Sharing History/Preserving Memories. Connecticut State Library. http://ctinworldwar1.org.

Segel, Robert G. "U.S. Colt Vickers Model of 1915." *Small Arms Defense Journal* 3, no. 1 (January 6, 2012). http://www.sadefensejournal.com/wp/?p=756.

Index